G-SUIT

G-SUIT

Pages from the log book of the Israel Air Force

MERAV HALPERIN
and
AHARON LAPIDOT

Translated by
Lawrence Rifkin

SPHERE BOOKS LIMITED

A SPHERE BOOK

First published in Great Britain by
Sphere Books Ltd 1990
Reprinted 1991

A number of the chapters are based on stories
that appeared in *The Israel Air Force Journal*
written by Gil Arbel, Elinoar Ben-Akiva,
Zvi Gutman, Ariel Goler, Ron Hadar,
Tamar Ze'evi, Eli Naveh and Uri Amit.

Typeset by Leaper & Gard Ltd, Bristol, England
Reproduced, printed and bound in Great Britain by
The Guernsey Press Co. Ltd, Guernsey, Channel Islands.

ISBN 0 7474 0466 6

Sphere Books Ltd
A Division of
Macdonald Group Ltd
165 Great Dover Street
London SE1 4YA

A member of Maxwell Macmillan Publishing Corporation

Foreword

There have been many portraits of the Israel Air Force. Its wartime accomplishments and its contributions to routine security have won it a world reputation. However, the personnel behind the Air Force's operations, the pilots and navigators, have mostly remained unknown. This book offers a glimpse into their world, a special world of special people.

This is a wide-ranging collection of personal stories. Some are well-known, at least in Israel, and others appear here for the first time. They have one thing in common; each is brought to the reader just as the pilot told it. Every story thus presents a personal and private point of view.

The stories appear chronologically and deal with aerial warfare in the jet age, from Israel's first jet-on-jet combat in 1955 right on through to today, the 1980s. This is not the official story of the Israel Air Force, but it certainly contains part of the human side of the air arm's biography. These personal stories are an overview of the changes in the Air Force over the years. The pilot of the 1980s is pitted against different challenges and objectives than was his counterpart of the 1950s. The modern aircraft the Air Force has integrated into its inventories, and the technological advances over the years, have changed the face of aerial warfare, and have given rise to a new type of Israeli pilot. The emphasis has shifted to teamwork as opposed to the spontaneous and personal battle of the past. This development led to a change of values among the ranks of Israeli aircrews, and there are those who see this as a factor in the more restrained spirit that characterizes the Air Force of today.

A number of these stories have appeared in *The Israel Air Force Journal*, and some were rewritten for this book. Six pilots provided us with stories they wrote themselves; we have left these in their original form in order to maintain the personal style of the authors.

While this book was being put together Brigadier General Asher Snir passed away. Before his death he handed over two stories he had written. One of them – 'Requiem for an Enemy' – beautifully characterizes all that can be said about aerial warfare and about the Israeli fighter pilot. This was the natural choice for the prologue.

Merav Halperin and Aharon Lapidot

Prologue
REQUIEM FOR AN ENEMY
Brigadier General Asher Snir

Independence Day, 1970. Very good reasons to be happy, not only for the Air Force, whose absolute superiority that year spread its wings over the whole Middle East, but also for myself. I had a good year.

At the close of Independence Day all the aircrews used to get together at one of the bases, see the usual five cultural programmes put on by the various wings, and afterwards alternate between dancing the Hora with hundreds of people and drinking as much whisky as possible, until everyone was soaked through and fuelled to the brim and the temperature had risen high enough to break down proteins. Things were still this way in 1970, and anyone who thought such a celebration inappropriate, when it happened once a year and for good reasons, had a lot to learn. And I admit to being guilty of drinking as I should have, and of my uniform becoming soaked from my own sweat and that of my partners in the never-ending Hora circle. And I admit to driving unconscious between Hatzor and Tel Nof. And I admit to not remembering exactly how I made it to bed sometime before morning.

It wasn't all that bad; the next day would be easy. We'd go down to the squadron only in the afternoon, see what was happening, leave a duo behind on alert, and head to the beach at Palmachim to splash around in the water. We wouldn't go near the aircraft at all because everyone would be on his face from the explosive mixture of the night before.

You don't fly this way – safety above all.

Tomorrow morning comes – which is to say afternoon – and I slowly wake up, put on my coveralls and high-top boots as a matter of routine, take a swimsuit and towel, and go down to the squadron to see that everything's okay, to do whatever has to be done, and to go to the beach. The troops gather slowly, mostly sitting around and getting organized with an amazing lack of efficiency and with eyes half-open. Amos Amir, the squadron commander, and Yitzhak Nir, remain behind on alert. Amos is the oldest of us, and his status keeps him from being one of the boys. And Yitzhak Nir, who came to us from the Jezreel Valley, is apparently in some kind of trauma.

Everyone is still dragging his feet, and there goes the siren. In one second this slow dance turns into a rhumba. Amos and Nir hop into a jeep and speed out to the intercept stand. Operations announces over the loudspeaker that this is a real scramble, and that they want another two pilots right away. Bathing suits and towels go flying in all directions and everyone runs, pushing to be in the second pair. But I run fastest and am the first in the tender with a G-suit and helmet, and go racing off to the aircraft half-dressed. We know things in the north have been hot since morning; but, at any rate, for years I have had a guiding principle: push every time and someday your reward will come.

Still in the rolling tender, I see that Amos has gotten his engine started, but Nir is having problems; there are too many mechanics busy around his Mirage, and there is no wake of exhaust gases churning from his engine. In another moment Nir will decide to switch aircraft, but if I hurry I'll reach the spare before he does; as Ran Pecker once taught me, there is no sentimentality in war. And he knew about war in airplanes better than anyone.

I run in an unfastened and flapping G-suit to Mirage No. 19, which I love more than all the rest. I climb the ladder and jump into the cockpit with my legs straight out. The mechanics are already on the aircraft before I have completely dropped in, and they are all over me to harness me in and hook up my cables and hoses. They are chosen for the intercept stand according to their quickness and energy. (If they had lived two hundred years ago they would have been a bunch of marauders.) They are also chosen according

4

to how many onions they can eat. The process of strapping in and hooking up is accompanied by light bruises. They, too, have been taught there is no sentimentality . . .

Within a minute I'm all strapped in, hooked up, started up, and rolling out to the runway where Amos is waiting; we'll head out together.

Afterburners, take-off, a sharp turn, and north to the Golan Heights.

On the way ground control says to hurry, that things are hot in the Golan; there is shelling, there have been attacks by enemy aircraft in the northern Heights and on the Hermon, and more of our formations are heading to the area.

The Heights are full of smoke, a sign that leaves no doubt there's a war going on. We patrol north and south, with eyes wide open and scanning. The small radar in the nose still hasn't found a MiG – there's no reason even to hope it will – and it gets the inattention it deserves.

Suddenly Amos says quickly and quietly, as if he hopes no one else will hear, 'Come with me.' He drops like a rock. Going down, his two large wing tanks fall away in spumes of fuel; I jettison mine too, not knowing exactly what he's going after. I do know we're diving on the western Hermon where there's a lot of smoke, and understand that Amos has apparently seen enemy aircraft on the attack.

The Hermon looms huge to our right and rises high above us, and we are straightening out over one of its western valleys when I finally see what's going on: a lone MiG-17 moving north, running home along the border area between Syria and Lebanon. He doesn't see us. I'm a little sad. Amos, who's about a thousand metres in front of me, will bring him down right away. It's not fair; the MiG is alone and out ahead; he doesn't see us, and doesn't know he's about to come up against a squadron commander and his deputy who between them have already closed down a squadron of MiGs and more. No, this isn't fair. The pilot is also flying a MiG-17, which is inferior to our Mirage. But this could turn into a sudden trap because at certain turning conditions, and at low to medium speeds, the MiG-17 is actually superior to the Mirage, and whoever dares to be enticed into these conditions will get screwed right royal.

Amos quickly closes in on the MiG, but once he's within range the Syrian breaks sharply up and to the side, showing that he saw us in time. The MiG has pulled a good manoeuvre, at the right place and right time. An excellent break. Amos climbs; I go in for a pass and see the MiG descending in a sharp turn towards the wadi he broke out of, presenting along the width of my windscreen its whole silhouette – the large swept-back wings, short nose and high tail above the round fuselage. I set up the gunsight and estimate the distance. Just before coming into range the MiG really twists around and descends some more.

Shit! This guy has ruined my pass. I pull out and Amos pulls in. The pilot in the MiG exploits these seconds to finish his descent to the valley floor, to straighten out to the north, and to gather the speed he'll need to continue. Not bad, this man in the MiG.

I climb and go inverted to see whether I'll have any more opportunities, or whether Amos will get him right now. Once again I see the MiG break just in time and right on the deck, frustrating Amos's pass beautifully. I'm on my way in.

As we head north the valley narrows, with towering walls on both sides; the rough terrain now takes the field as the fourth player of this battle, and woe to him who forgets this.

The Syrian again breaks at the right place and time. I rise up and look down on him, faster and more powerful but far from able to get in a good shot. This guy is flying lower than anyone else I've seen; he knows where and when to look, gets an excellent idea of the picture, and has the proper powers of concentration to fly so low, to think correctly, to judge when to do things, and not make any mistakes. This guy is flying really well, not just according to Arab Air Force standards, but by any standards. And I come to understand that we've found ourselves a real opponent, as good as any we know, and that this fight will apparently be completely different.

At about this time a similar thought almost certainly passes through the Syrian's mind, something like: 'I've been seen; the two of them know how to fly, and if I'm not perfect things won't end so well. I'll have to fly like I've never flown before, and like I hope I'll never have to again. Let's see what happens.'

You can almost see the Syrian throw the book out the window, remaining alone with his machine, without his rules and regulations or the things they had taught him, things better suited for people less talented and for situations less difficult. Alone, man and machine.

I've related to myself with a strange mixture of feelings since I found myself in a wadi on the Hermon in the spring of 1970. The Syrian had got through to me, and I got carried away. He heated me up, and I boiled over. He fought us with no holds barred, and I fought him the same way. He took chances the likes of which we had never seen, with me right after him. He flew disregarding all the limits, and so did I. One shouldn't have to fight this way; this wasn't how I had learned. One should never fly at such a high level of risk, where only success separates you from criminal negligence. But something told me with absolute certainty that on this day, and with this man, this was the way it had to be, and there was no way he could return home and tell everyone in the officers' club how he was jumped by two Mirages, yet got away safely because he flew too low for the frightened Jews. To this day I don't know if it was the right thing to do, and no one can tell me.

The fight lasted eight-and-a-half minutes; aside from the wildness it was flawless both on our side and his. That part of the brain responsible for planning, for decisions and for judgement worked fine; it knew to differentiate between what was dangerous but correct, and what was an outright mistake.

I remember nothing of the view, save for obstacles and opportunities. I remember my surroundings as an eight-and-a-half minute time-tunnel with a sequence of entrances and exits, three bursts of fire that missed, and a very hard time. I remember him sitting at least once at the bottom of my sight, with me unable to lower it on him even a single millimetre because we were between the trees, and he had already dropped down a few more terrace levels. I remember checking my fuel a few times, and checking whether someone was behind. I remember maintaining the right speeds, and dropping my centreline tank just when it showed empty. I remember a number of radio co-ordinations and clearing the rear with Amos, who I think was just as hot under the collar. I remember the Syrian pulling up his nose along with me on one of his pull-outs, and the two of us rising out of the valley together, spilling over with cold anger. I remember Amos, who was watching over everything, saying, 'Look out, he's going up with you;' and myself, alive and alert like never before, knowing the exact speed the man in the MiG had on his gauge, and that he was bluffing. I remember the heavy breathing and the sweat pouring off me, and my wonderful No. 19 going along with me, with all its power and all its fire, smooth and strong and rejoicing in battle.

And so we're heading farther north, three mental cases wedded in a Catholic union, not knowing who'll make it and who won't.

The missile at my wingtip, an American Sidewinder, hums every once in a while, telling me it sees the MiG. But I am well acquainted with missiles – especially this one, as I did the delivery tests – and know perfectly the crookedness of its flight path and how the steering balances its centre of gravity. I know I shouldn't launch one at this altitude because it would simply hit the ground right in front of me if I didn't give it enough space to sink before it began to home in and gain height.

For a long time I stay away from the Sidewinder, and justifiably so, until in one of my climbs I see the MiG is about to cross a rather wide valley lying precisely perpendicular to his flight path. The guy in the MiG can't know this because he sees just the ridge in front. Amos is almost within range, but the Syrian is still at work and breaks nicely between the trees. Now's the time: the valley will allow the missile to sink, and I have to plan things so the missile will reach the nadir of its flight path right there in the valley and rise up in time to hit the Syrian before he crosses the ridge on the far side. I decide it's possible, but have to hurry.

I don't go back down to the MiG; instead I stay up and close in to 800 metres – the heart of the missile's flight envelope – and see the silhouette of the silver MiG, looking like a flying fish, again running from Amos's Mirage and twisting away to the north, and home. The MiG runs right over the boulders, writhing inside the valley which has now become a ravine, and goes along it towards the ridge.

Now!

My sights are right on the distant tailpipe; I get the missile's battle cry, and before the Syrian figures out that the valley floor is about to fall away, I fire. A sharp whoosh from the wingtip and the missile is on its way. But it's twisting (all missiles are like this, the physics of ˉteering) and running towards the top of the closer ridge, its black exhaust pipe skidding just above it. In a moment we'll see whether it will make it over the ridge, or remain behind on one of the boulders.

The MiG crosses the ridge first. What are the Syrian's thoughts when he sees the protective ground slip away, not to return until the other side of the valley? Maybe he thinks nothing at all. Or maybe he thinks, 'One of the Mirages has pulled out and poses no threat, while the other has slipped too far back to be a problem. By the time the two of them make further contact the valley will end and the ground will come back. And aside from this, they've been on me for eight minutes now, and in another minute they'll be low on fuel and have to leave. And maybe help will arrive. It'll be all right, I'm in good shape.'

Two seconds behind him the missile also clears the ridge, no doubt setting the world record for low-flight missiles. After this it continues to drop a little more towards the valley floor, and then begins to rise, homing in well and stable, moving along quickly and poised for a direct hit.

Something causes the Syrian to do the last thing he'll ever do – maybe he sees a distant part of the missile's smoke trail, maybe he feels uncomfortable about something; maybe he's started getting suspicious; no one will ever know – but when the missile is fifty metres away the guy begins to break to the right, still within the valley. However, things are too close, and it's too late. The missile easily follows the break, arms its ten kilogram warhead, and disappears beneath the descending right wing.

After this everything comes at once. The last second of this brave and talented man is still with me; the missile with its thin feather of smoke vanishing under the wing; the large, orange explosion, almost certainly a direct hit; the wing tearing off at the root; the fast and uncontrollable roll in the direction of the missing wing; the jerking turn of the one-winged fuselage – and, afterwards, unavoidably, the explosive meeting of the broken MiG and the steep, far wall of the valley, with the orange-black mushroom blossoming, quite ugly, from among the greenery.

It is really far off, maybe 700 metres away. Maybe because of this, my victory and the Syrian's death are of secondary importance to the overall experience, and a somewhat disappointing ending to the combat. I don't remember rejoicing, not at the moment of bringing him down, nor on the long way home; just total exhaustion and drying sweat.

I make my victory roll above the squadron, carrying out a long tradition, and with great care and the concentration of a greenhorn, I land and taxi to the stand. I shut down the engine, turn off the switches, unfasten myself, rise to climb down to the small and happy crowd of mechanics, female clerks, and pilots, and then realize that I need all my strength to stand up in the cockpit, and that underneath my soaked G-suit are legs I am no longer familiar with.

There were debriefings and the screening of the gun camera film, and some murmuring when the trees appeared at aircraft level. I don't remember much of this. Afterwards they said they knew who the guy was: a well-known lieutenant colonel, an excellent pilot, the man sent to lay down the sonic boom over Haifa. It was said they gave him a state funeral in Damascus and posthumous promotion to colonel. And I knew, as we know the truly important things, that he deserved both. Then they said no, maybe he had fallen before Babbin's guns the same morning, and that the guy I met over the Hermon was some unknown pilot. Today it's clear they didn't know. But it's not important.

A famous hero or an unknown at the beginning of the road, he deserved one thing, and to this day I hope he got it: that he was killed in the explosion of the missile itself and didn't live through the last second before the crash, and thus didn't know he lost the battle.

Chapter 1
SEASON OF THE JETS

The first Arab–Israeli jet-to-jet combat took place in 1955 when Egyptian Vampires penetrated Israel's air space. Colonel (Res) Aharon Yoeli, then a twenty-six-year-old Israel Air Force captain and Meteor pilot, attacked the two Egyptian jets and shot them down, one after the other. For this feat he won the Ot Haoz, *Israel's second highest decoration for bravery.*

The story of this dogfight actually began two years before, in 1953, the year the IAF established a Meteor squadron, its first gunnery. Much labour went into this, a lot of toil and sweat, a routine of tough training only after which did we get out to do the real thing. During the entire two-year period we remained untried in operational sorties. It was a time of absolute quiet in the skies. In fact, up until this dogfight I had had no experience whatsoever under true combat conditions.

Menahem Bar was squadron commander, and Joe Alon and I were the two deputies. Menahem introduced discipline, order, precision and regularity into our training. 'It's not enough to get on his tail,' he would say, 'you've also got to know how to hit him.' For two years I lived this maxim.

Our aircraft did not have radar; they had World War Two-style gunsights for which you had to provide the range to target. We had to wait two seconds until the data entered the sights on the way in to the hit. 'Diamonds', they called those little dots of light that closed in on the target. A real

11

joke. A gold ring in a pig's nose, only reversed; a primitive gunsight in an advanced aircraft.

The dogfight took place during a period of retaliatory ground actions. Before a paratroop raid on Gaza they placed two Meteors and four pilots on alert at Hatzor. We went down there the day before the excitement, on 31 August, which was my birthday. We rotated the alerts, with the pair on duty being changed every few hours.

The next day the other pair was on, and just then, as in all the good stories, the alarm bell went off. My Number Two was Yehoash Chatto (Tzidon). A half-second was enough for us to give each other an understanding look before sprinting the 200 metres between the squadron and the aircraft. We beat the duty pair and established an incontrovertible fact: it would be us, and not them.

The aircraft were prepared for night alert, and this would have great bearing on what was to come. With the sights set for night, the illumination was dimmed and the range was set at just 100 metres. We had no time to make any changes because the moment we were settled in the cockpits they yelled, 'Scramble!'

Seven in the morning. We've got night sights, and take off to the west into rather overcast skies. The clouds are at 4000 to 6000 feet. We can barely see through them; the best we can do is get a quick look through the holes. We climb to the cloud peaks, where ground control catches up with us. 'Enemy aircraft within our air space, north of the Gaza Strip, flying south from Ashkelon.'

I head east so we'll be up-sun. We fly on and on, and then Chatto says, 'Two aircraft, three o'clock low.' I look and see two Vampires, one close to me, the other farther away. Immediately I pull away, close the throttles and start after the Vampire that's a little behind. They are both flying toward Egypt at 2000 feet. Apparently, they'd been to see what was going on in the Gaza Strip area, had patrolled a bit, and were now starting home.

I close in on the aircraft, quite annoyed that my sights are set for night and there's no time to deal with it. I come in very, very slowly, right behind him, cock the cannons and press the trigger. We have a system where every fifth shell is a tracer so we can see where we're firing; I just want to see if I'm on target, and hold off. If I shoot him down now he'll

12

drop right on the dining room at Kibbutz Karmia.

I close in to 150 metres, a beautiful range, and open up with real firepower: four 20mm cannons. And just like in those dozens of arduous practice fights – the entire, great secret of success – I hit him square on. The shells start eating away at his left wing and move to the wing root, the whole thing ending with a terrible explosion.

We break left as I revel in the first victory – for me, for the squadron, for the aircraft – and the second Vampire turns towards us. We pull up hard, and the Vampire turns back to the south and tries to get away. The Vampire is slower than a Meteor but is far more manoeuvrable; it dives to gain speed and I run after it at full power. We're nearing the border. Kibbutz Erez is right underneath us; I was a member of this kibbutz, and I want to bring it down in our fields.

The Vampire tries to break to the east. I'm about 200 metres away. He rolls at low level – about 500 feet – and I look on in disbelief, waiting for him to finish his aerobatics. I think to myself that maybe the Russians had taught him to flip around like this in a dogfight.

Because I don't have a gunsight I decide to aim by instinct. I position the aircraft ahead of his line of flight and open fire; whatever happens will happen. As with the best-placed aim the first burst goes right into the cockpit. The aircraft crashes west of Erez.

We pull up. My elation is clouded by just one thought: too bad he didn't jump. I would have wanted to sit with him later in a bar. But neither of them jumped. And the thought that there was nothing I could have done goes through my head.

At 7:20 we were already home. The whole way back Chatto was bubbling with excitement. 'What a festivity! You can't imagine. I saw it all, the smoke, the explosions. What a performance!' He didn't shut his mouth the whole way back to Hatzor. And at Hatzor, the epitome of pilot swagger; a wild buzz, a pull-up, two pretty rolls, and a perfect landing.

Elation soared to the heavens. The Air Force hadn't had an air victory since '48. The Hatzor commander at the time was Leslie Easterman, a reserved Briton, cold as a fish. He came up to me and said quietly, in a heavy British accent, 'I understand you shot down two planes.' I went, 'Uh-uh,' gushing with joy, and then he said, 'Are you quite sure they weren't ours?' His timing couldn't have been better.

13

The next day Air Force Commander Dan Tolkovsky took us to Ben-Gurion. The Old Man wouldn't let Chatto go, trying to convince him to Hebraicize his surname. (Ben-Gurion, whose surname was Hebrew for 'son of a lion cub', had been born David Green and believed all Israelis should Hebraicize their names.) Tolkovsky, with his surname stood to the side and cringed. Ben-Gurion bombarded us with super-professional questions: 'I heard you were careful with the sun. Where were they flying? How did you shoot down the first one? With cannons? Tell me, tell me.' I was amazed.

This was another era. My gun camera film was shown in a Petah Tikva movie house; my parents' home filled up with flowers; there were congratulatory messages in the newspapers, and the mayor of Ashkelon presented me with a watch in gratitude for not having shot down the aircraft over his city.

My wife, who had been informed of the Vampire downings while I was still in the air, characteristically asked, 'And what about the Egyptian pilots?' When they told her, she replied, 'Too bad, their poor mothers.'

Chapter 2
HOME FROM THE DESERT

During the 1956 Sinai Campaign a Mystere fighter flown by Benny Peled (later Major General and commander of the IAF) was hit during an attack on Ras Nasrani. Peled ejected from his stricken aircraft and hid in the desert. Major (Res) Avraham Greenbaum, then a Piper Cub pilot, was sent to the rescue. This daring mission won him a commendation.

I had been released from active duty half a year before and had already chalked up two accidents in fighters, so they made me a Piper pilot in the reserves. This was during a period of anti-terrorist activity, and as a result we were mobilized at regular intervals. Now they told us we were going down to Eilat. I sensed nothing extraordinary, and it was only later in the evening that I found out this was to be the beginning of the Sinai Campaign.

I was assigned to the 9th Brigade, commanded by the late Avraham Yoffe, and was to make patrol flights over Sinai to ensure that the brigade's route of advance was clear. By this time the brigade infantry column had passed the halfway mark between Eilat and Sharm e-Sheikh, with me out ahead and guiding it from above. Accompanying me the whole time was Gadi, large in build, with eagle eyes and a wonderful disposition, and well-known in the relatively small and family-like Israel Defence Forces of 1956 as a top recce soldier.

During a reconnaissance flight on the fifth day of battle, my squadron commander informed me that two pilots had bailed out over the desert between Sharm and Ras Nasrani. He had tried to reach me from the ground in Eilat but my Piper radio was too weak for the range. With no other choice my commander went up in another Piper, and only then did he succeed in making contact. He inquired about my fuel and warned me about anti-aircraft fire. I chuckled. There was no need for ack-ack to bring down a Piper; a rifle bullet would have been enough to leave us in the desert forever.

I climbed to 10,000 feet, the Piper's performance ceiling, while picturing the faces of the two downed fliers – Benny Peled, commander of a Mystere squadron, and Yonatan Atkes, a Mustang pilot. I was not told that another Piper had already looked for the two men, and had failed.

When I levelled off at the Piper's maximum altitude, I was awestruck. Before me was an intoxicating picture; the arrow-like tip of Sinai, the Gulf of Suez and the Red Sea. The beauty dazzled my eyes. I had never seen this place before.

I started a circular, gliding descent, going down to 8000, 7000, 6000 feet, but didn't see a thing. At about 4000 feet I saw a black spot that could have been the result of an explosion or a crashed plane. I descended further and saw the wreckage of an aircraft. It was northwest of Ras Nasrani, on a desert plateau that ran up to the mountains. I figured that if the pilot had bailed out, he had to be close by. I continued to descend and at a very low altitude noticed two figures. I began to glide towards them, but when I was close enough I saw they weren't ours: Egyptian soldiers with Carl Gustav submachine-guns. I hesitated over whether to get out of there or continue, and chose a third option: I began to dive on them at full power. They lay down on the ground. Gadi had an Uzi in his hand and I told him, 'If they don't shoot, neither will we.' Today, when I think about this, it was really strange. The Egyptians lay there motionless, seemingly indifferent to what was going on. They never tried to aim at us, nor did they try to run for cover.

I pulled left, towards the south. It was getting late; the sun was low in the west, with me between it and Ras Nasrani. Gadi was searching for any movement in the desert. Turning southward I noticed something white flapping at the foot of the hills. At first I had reservations – I was afraid of an

16

Egyptian ambush. The whole thing looked suspicious; the two Egyptians were still lying there and I feared they were trying to lure me into a trap. But I closed in and saw someone else lying there, waving a white cloth. Gadi took a look through the field glasses and excitedly exclaimed, 'It's him! It's got to be him!' I was still hesitant, but decided to circle at low altitude. I glanced at the figure and didn't recognize him. He was wearing one of our flight coveralls, but this was not proof enough. I dropped down some more and still didn't recognize him. At the time Benny Peled was a squadron leader, well-known in the IAF, and I was certain I would recognize him if I saw him. I decided on one last try before I allowed myself to be convinced that this was a trap. I flew past a third time, opened the window, stuck my head out and yelled 'Weidenfeld!' – Benny's name before he Hebraicized it to Peled. His face was red, dusty and contorted. Only from this close could I recognize him. I was to discover that he had suffered facial injuries while bailing out, and this was why I couldn't recognize him. It was the first time anyone in the IAF had used an ejection seat, so I didn't know the signs of having ejected.

I flew over the plateau and started searching for a flat area to land. The wadi was littered with head-sized rocks and there was a risk my tyres would burst from the landing. I touched down as gently as I could and turned off the engine. Benny remained where he was; I wondered why he didn't scramble toward us. Gadi jumped from the Piper and raced over, while I kept my eyes on the Egyptian soldiers; they still hadn't reacted to what was going on – as if there was a gentlemen's agreement. You don't shoot at us, we won't shoot at you.

I ran after Gadi. He reached Benny – and only then did I understand that Benny had been hurt. Gadi heaved him over his shoulder, and the two of them crashed to the ground. I had to laugh. Benny was very heavy at the time and his weight was too much for Gadi. Together we shuffled to the plane, Benny between us with his arms over our shoulders. He was limping heavily, having broken a leg on hitting the ground. We placed him on a stretcher on the Piper's back seat. Then Gadi and I got in. I started the engine and tried to shut the door. It wouldn't close – the cabin was overloaded. I considered dumping the radio and putting a machine-gun burst into it, but just then the door snapped shut. We took off.

The Egyptians were still lying on the ground, apparently in shock. Benny was very tense. He had been lying in the sun for hours before we found him. Over the water he loosened up and returned to his old self. It was already almost totally dark, and we were unable to make radio contact with the rear in Eilat, but Benny was worried about other things. 'Why did you turn the engine off when you landed? What if it wouldn't start? And why did you make three passes?' That was Benny. He was lying in the back, writhing in agony and grumbling, 'You're doing your checklist too high.' Not a word about himself. The minute the danger had passed, he was criticizing. The only human thing he said during the flight was that he was going to make me an honorary pilot of his squadron. He kept his promise; when I received my commendation he organized a fly-past of four Mysteres in formation over the awards ceremony.

I have made more dangerous flights, but this was one where you got to harvest the fruits. To save a pilot entails an element of emotion. I felt honoured to have done something, not necessarily in battle: a simple flight from which you return elated.

Time has seen the story of this flight embellished with the folklore of heroism. Ezer Weizman always embarrasses me by telling everyone that they fired at me and that I landed between the bullets. I don't know about that. For me it's enough that I was able to bring a pilot home.

Chapter 3
NIGHT RECCE

*IAF Major (Res) Reuven Harel and Lieutenant Colonel (Res)
Yossi Sarig undertook the Israel Air Force's first night photo
reconnaissance mission in 1962. The objective was the Cairo-
West airfield. The flight to Egypt and back was flown at low
level by two pilots sharing a Vautour.*

After the 1958 raid on PLO headquarters in Tunis, Minister
Without Portfolio Ezer Weizman (who in 1962 was IAF
commander) called me and said, 'What's all this noise about
Tunis? What's the big deal about flying an F-16 and
dropping some bombs? What you two did twenty years ago,
that was something!'

'Nice to hear,' I answered, 'but as far as I'm concerned just
flying an F-16, with all its sophistication, is a very big deal.'

In 1962, it was decided to undertake the IAF's first night
recce mission, which at the time was a rather revolutionary
step. Like every important decision it was made out of
necessity: it was impossible to obtain the desired information
in daylight because of the fear of interception. The only thing
left was the night option which, by the concepts of the time,
was the epitome of daring and danger.

Naturally the job fell to us, the Vautour squadron. At the
time we specialized chiefly in recce flights, but only in
daylight. Ya'acov Agassi was our commander, and Reuven
and I were his deputies. Ezer Weizman wanted Agassi to fly

19

the mission alone but, surprisingly, Agassi said there was a scheduled roster. This was the first exceptional thing about the sortie: Agassi agreed someone else should get a chance to do it.

For routine recce flights, two crew members would be sent: a pilot and a navigator. When the night mission was called, I suggested that two pilots fly it. Why two pilots? First, because Reuven and I were arguing over whose turn it was according to the roster. Second, we didn't trust any navigator with such a complicated mission. I then suggested that I go as navigator, and that Reuven fly. This combination calmed the Air Force brass, and convinced them the whole thing could work.

We knew this would be a difficult and dangerous mission. At the time, night recce photography was technically complicated; for illumination we had to drop a flare, and only then would the shutter open. This required us to be directly over target. Navigation would also have to be precise. Back then there were no navigation computers and one had to rely solely on maps. And as map-reading at night was impossible, we had to find an alternative. Most of all, there was the fear that accompanies all low-altitude night work – of flying into the ground. For this reason it was important to have two pilots. When we got the go-ahead for the mission, Reuven and I took full responsibility for the aircraft and the mission's success.

The recce flight's farthest and westernmost objective was Cairo-West airfield. On the way back we were to photograph other fields: Inshas (where there were nightfighters), Abu Suweir and Mansura, all of which were in the Delta. We took our map and, using phosphorescent ink, marked those cities and villages that stood out most. We figured that by locating their lights we would have our reference points along the way. We chose a night with a full moon in mid-sky to provide enough light for us to find our way. That night would be 23 January 1962, and until zero-hour all we had to do was practise.

The squadron planned the mission down to the last detail. The range involved was long, even by Vautour standards, and the flight would take an hour each way. We planned to fly a straight line over the Mediterranean to the Libyan desert, cross the coast, go south and then east to the field. A good part of the flight would be over the sea. This presented an additional problem: the sea is monotonous, and when flying over it at low altitude for a long time there is no way of discerning drift. It's also very tiring; there's a tendency to doze off and lose your sense of height. And the fear of discovery by enemy radar forced us to fly as low as we dared.

Reuven and I flew together on only one low-level, night-practice flight before the mission; the others were flown separately. I faced the challenge of adjusting to the navigator's cockpit. I sat there for a few hours to acclimatize myself, to study the switches and learn the systems. The cockpit was closed on all sides; you entered from above, the hatch closing like a cover, and sat there hunched forward. Your field of view ahead and to the sides was very limited. But the desire to go on this mission was so powerful that I forced myself to get used to sitting in the dark chamber that was the Vautour navigator's cockpit.

We got the impression that everyone was waiting for the results of our flight. We knew that during the mission everybody would be sitting waiting in the Air Force war room, known as the 'pit'. If we succeeded it would be a real breakthrough. If we failed it would mean disgrace.

We took off at one o'clock at night in complete radio silence and flew in a straight line for forty-five minutes – only to discover that we had no idea where we were. Unknown to us, the compass was off by one degree; instead of hitting the coast we were still over water. The plan was to identify landfall by the coastal lights. Three minutes before we expected to reach land we saw small, scattered lights, but as we approached we realized they were fishing boats! We knew we'd gone wrong, but had no idea of our location, and the hour at which we were supposed to cross the coast went by.

We finally hit land, two minutes late. In a jet, this was a tremendous deviation and we didn't know where we had gone wrong. We turned south, according to plan, not really knowing where we were going. The whole, beautiful scheme for identification by the lights on the ground now went for naught, and we were under tremendous pressure.

Our sense of error increased as we reached the Nile delta, which was blanketed by haze. Combined haze and moonlight can be fatal when it comes to vision, and now all the cities, villages and fields looked alike. Everything was soft and blurred and there was no way to determine where we were.

According to our map, we should have been able to identify something new every minute. But nothing I had marked could be seen on the ground. We continued to fly over the desert for a few minutes, sure we would never hit any of our reference points and were heading right into a fine mess. Then Reuven and I began to argue over whether we were left or right of our planned course, not knowing if we should turn east or west. I cut the dispute short by saying, 'Give me some quiet so I can think!'

I was ashamed and began to panic. It was unthinkable to screw up on such a mission, and I was on the verge of despair. The trouble we had pinpointing our location was a terrible surprise for me. But in the middle of my hysteria it suddenly dawned on me: we had to correct to the east because we had been flying west. I decided we should continue straight until we met the desert road, then follow it east to Cairo-West. We began navigating like infantrymen: find the road and it will get you where you want to go.

After a few nerve-wracking minutes we hooked up with the road and continued along it to the field. What a relief! The sin of having screwed up the navigation was lifted from my shoulders. We pulled up to 4000 feet, did two quick passes and continued on to the other fields. On the way we made a low pass to break the tension – and wake up the Cairenes. We arrived at Inshas, did two photo runs, another pass to wake up their interceptor pilots, and then moved on. There was a bit of anti-aircraft fire, but by this point we were already far away – very far away.

Chapter 4
OPENING BLOW

Almost all of the Israel Air Force's fighter aircraft participated in the opening attack wave of the 1967 Six Day War. Colonel (Res) Oded Merom, author of the first segment of this chapter, was deputy commander of a Mirage squadron, Brigadier General B was a Vautour pilot, and Major General Avihu Bin-Nun, now IAF commander and whose story closes the chapter, was a Mystere pilot.

Col (Res) Oded Merom I go up the ladder, rest my helmet on the ejection seat, and settle heavily into the cockpit. Gideon, the smiling mechanic, gets busy hooking up harnesses, removing safety pins from the ejection seat detonators and fixing the parachute straps. His face looks different today. With a worried expression, he follows my movements, which are familiar to him. I lift my right arm and he lengthens the right harness, and so on, through the days, months and years of practice and combat flights.

At this hour of morning on 5 June the cockpit is cool and pleasant. The metal, cold from the night air, is startling to the touch and wakes you up.

Preparations for the flight had begun at an early hour. All of us had gone to the briefing room and taken our places. Amos, the squadron leader, gave the briefing, which was short, clear and to the point. Strict instructions: 'All aircraft will maintain absolute radio silence from take-off until zero-hour, which is set for 0745 hours. Under no circumstances is the radio silence to be broken, not even for accident or malfunction. Anyone whose aircraft has aborted while still on the ground will not take off; there are no spare planes. In case of malfunction during take-off, get off the runway and into the ploughed field to allow the others to go. The emergency crews are on full alert. They'll try to help ...'

One last time Gideon checks harnesses, ejection-seat pins, controls and gauges. He slides his hand along the oxygen hose, glances over his shoulder to see whether the system is working like it should, and steps down one rung on the ladder. His head is level with mine and I smile at him; he smiles back in embarrassment, descends from the ladder, and steps away from the aircraft.

That's it. I'm alone.

I press a button to close the canopy and quiet pervades the cockpit. The people outside seem distant and foreign. From now on I'm on my own; no one can help me get the job done. The fate of the mission and of the formation I'll be leading against Cairo-West will be in my hands. The airfield, so we were told, is home to giant Tupolev Tu-16 bombers and is on the edge of the desert west of Cairo.

Earlier this morning, before I put on my coveralls, I went into the kids' room. My two children were fast asleep. Six-year-old Guy and my two-year-old daughter, Nitzan, had no idea what was about to happen; they were scheduled to be taken by bus to a hotel in Natania with the rest of the families from the air base at this very moment. I didn't kiss them for fear of waking them. Now I'm sorry. Will I get to kiss them again?

The mechanics start up the generator with a great crash of thunder, the needles on the gauges quiver and settle into place. A quick glance at the instrument panel: all normal. Outside, Gideon raises his right arm and gives me the thumbs-up.

Mechanically, I press the starter button. The familiar noise of compressed air released from the starter bottles, and the needles show high revs. So routine and familiar.

This morning we'll take off on the mission we've been practising for many years. From the day the wings were pinned on my chest we have practised raids against airfields. We've gone over the textbooks in every possible way. We've learned to attack runways from high altitude and from low altitude. We've learned and flown attack missions in pairs, foursomes, and flights of six. We've attacked at first light, when the sun blinds the defenders on the ground, and at twilight, when raiding aircraft would be lost in the falling darkness. We've learned to aim bombs at the intersection of runways to put a field completely out of action. We've learned to protect ourselves from enemy interceptors.

The time has now come. Everyone will show what they've learned, and what they can do. For the first time in the history of the Air Force everything is being done by the book; this morning some two hundred aircraft, loaded with bombs, will take off to destroy the airfields of Egypt, and afterwards perhaps those of other enemy states.

The engine is running like it should. With annoying slowness – but efficiently – the mechanics again and again check the ordnance suspended from the aircraft. Underneath my Mirage are two 500-kilogram bombs; with two 1000-kilo drop tanks, the payload comes to three tons. Flying fast at low altitude, the Mirage will perform very sluggishly.

Final cockpit checks before heading out to the runway; a pull and twist on the handle and the parking brake is released. With a shudder, the heavy airplane begins to taxi on the runway. The radio is completely silent; no one dares even a click to find out if his radio works at all.

Aircraft that arrived a few minutes ago are already waiting in take-off position, the pilots all lost in their own worlds. Once more one of them checks his maps. Once again his buddy goes over the arming procedure. Time drags. Each minute more aircraft taxi to take-off position. For a moment it seems there will be a traffic jam, but each plane has its designated position; everyone knows exactly which minute he's to mount the runway, run up his engine, and take off. Each pilot looks for his leader, whom he'll identify by tail number. Noisy tailplanes of dozens of aircraft kick up a lot of dust, but inside the cockpits there is total silence. Only the needles move: fuel indicator, engine gauges and flight instruments. Lights flash nervously to show the switching order for fuel tanks and the arming sequence for the bombs.

The great take-off begins. The aircraft on the runway start their runs pair by pair. Dust, noise and, most of all, excitement, rise into the air. The planes are taking off. Now no one will stop the process.

In my imagination I see hundreds of aircraft taking off from all the air bases: Ouragans, Mysteres, Super Mysteres, Vautours and Mirages. Every available plane in the Air Force, all loaded with bombs, rockets and cannons. There is no power on earth that can stop these aircraft from rising towards their targets; such is this great machine. Everyone who can take off, will. Whoever arrives over target will attack. Those who attack and make it back will land. And only then will it be possible to learn the outcome of the raid.

A kind of cocoon envelops me, and everything is done as it was in the never-ending training sessions. We're on the runway. All the aircraft of my formation are ready. I release the brakes and the plane is shoved forward by the thrust of the afterburner. Speed builds up: 145 knots. The aircraft dances a little and then rises into the air. The wheels fold with a light thump. I'm airborne, at tree-top height.

Heading for the sea. We'll fly a long way out over the Mediterranean and afterwards turn south to cross into Egypt from the north. Over the water there's no way to identify my position; the idea is to maintain precise heading by compass. There is no help from ground contours; over the sea we're on our own. The minutes go by and there's only one kind of scenery; waves, blue and threatening; a blue desert stretching to the horizon.

The aircraft claw forward at low altitude. I'm tense coming up to the minute we'll turn left, south towards Egypt. The left turn will bring us onto course for the Nile delta, to the Cairo-West airfield. We're headed toward the Egyptian coast. Offshore an occasional Egyptian fishing boat can be seen; the fishermen are busy with their work and don't raise their eyes. They could never guess what is happening.

The strip of golden sand appearing before us on the horizon is Bardawil lagoon, which we have to cross. The lagoon bustles with fishing boats and the fishermen, folding their nets after a night's work, wave hello. A symphony of blue water and golden sand, a pastoral scene in all that meets the eye. And above it all we fly in thundering war machines carrying a load of destruction to the enemy heartland.

A few seconds later and Bardawil lagoon disappears behind us. In the distance we can already see the Suez Canal, merchant vessels and fishing boats with white sails. The canal also goes by and vanishes, and the view now changes to green carpeting with small squares of cultivated fields. Interspersed between them are farmhouses, small and white. Only a few minutes till the airfield.

The aircraft flies steadily on course and I try to identify my position by the map and the villages on the way, but without success. All fields look the same, as would two grains of rice, and all the villages have the same layout. The only thing to do is something tried and true – fly by compass and clock.

We pass north of Cairo. Just a few more minutes. I stretch in the narrow seat and try to relieve the stiffness that has built up during the flight. The formation is spread out on both sides, and we all know that within moments we'll be in the middle of hell.

The final minute. This is it. There's a pillar of smoke in the distance sent up by a formation that struck a few minutes before.

We arrive precisely at our point-of-attack approach. Radio silence is broken; dryly I announce: 'Full power.' The pilots react adroitly and the formation spreads out into an arrowhead. We pull back on our sticks – and we're attacking.

All our senses are tensed as the aircraft, loaded to the limit, rise: 7000 feet, 9000 feet and I roll and dive towards the runway. The formation follows.

The dots of light in the bombsight shine like diamonds against the black asphalt of the runway. I notice aircraft burning on the ground, and out of the corner of my eye I see Tupolevs standing undamaged at the edge of the field. A push of the bomb-release button and two bombs are on their way towards the runway. The whole formation releases its bombs on the designated targets, and we wheel over the desert at low altitude to go back and strafe the giant bombers.

I come in out of a shallow dive and the gunsight settles on a shining Tupolev. My finger squeezes the trigger on the column, the cannons roar and a burst of 30mm shells rips through the bomber. It immediately catches fire and thick, black smoke begins to rise. A second and a third strafing run, and black pillars of smoke rise from all corners of the field. Mission accomplished. In addition to bombing the runway we've destroyed five Tu-16s.

We head out on the long and dangerous road home.

Brig Gen B Our Vautour squadron was assigned a special mission: Beni Suef airfield in the southern delta, with its concentrations of Tupolev Tu-16s waiting to bomb large civilian centres in Israel. The Egyptians were sure that no Israeli plane had the range to reach this base. To us the Tupolevs symbolized one of the greatest wartime threats to national morale.

I was assigned to the first foursome. We got set for take-off but, during final checks on the runway, a malfunction was discovered in one of the aircraft. We went as a threesome. Start-up; 21 tons, a fully-armed aircraft; take-off – and this time it isn't an exercise.

We crossed the border near the Ramon crater. When the terrain changes from the familiar to the hostile, your thoughts centre on the course, the timetable, control and execution. It was clear to every pilot that success depended on each of us, and that victory or defeat hung on accuracy.

After a few seconds we were confronted by a strange sight that is still fresh in my mind: a huge column of Egyptian armour and vehicles strung out before us in the Nakhl area; hundreds of soldiers standing nearby, shading their eyes and excitedly waving hello. At this moment I knew the war was won.

We crossed the Gulf of Suez. How narrow it was, and these waters, fiercely blue, were teeming with sharks. Now we were on the other side and desert again. We sped towards the Nile Valley. Agricultural land, then water again, a bit murky, with sailboats. It looked like a painting, not at all like war.

Towards the target area we were greeted by an unwelcome morning fog. No practice or sophisticated preparations would have helped in such a situation. If we couldn't identify the target through fog or clouds, the mission couldn't be carried out. We flew on – and got lucky; the target area was not socked in. I climbed to find the objective, and the field materialized before my eyes; long, wide concrete runways and, on them, the aircraft – exposed, uncamouflaged, and gleaming like aluminium pots and pans.

Two bombing passes on the runways. No wind, a wide runway, a huge, easy target; all the bombs bullseyes. And then for the strafing passes. It was a little strange firing at real aircraft instead of targets at the practice range. Mixed feelings. After all the years and flight experience, you develop a kind of respect for an airplane, and here you're ready to fire at real ones and reduce them to ashes.

The ack-ack was very light; we had surprised them completely. On the last pass I felt a sudden impact and the aircraft tilted into a climb: my flight controls had been hit. Instinctively I pushed the stick forward and reduced power. I was able to regain control but was afraid that I might have to eject out there in the desert; from there to the Land of Israel could be a matter of forty years. Then my flight leader caught up, scanned my plane and said the damage was minimal. We left the area behind and climbed to altitude. Homeward.

Maj Gen Avihu Bin-Nun I can't remember any flight that provoked such a sense of responsibility and seriousness as the one assigned to the pilots of those formations that took off on the morning of 5 June 1967. For the previous two or three weeks we had trained in the same formation and practised the same mission. We knew how to do it with our eyes closed: a blowout – get off the runway; engine malfunction – abort; anything but don't block the runway. If all went as it should, we'd fly very low over the sea, cross Bardawil and attack Fayid airfield. Three Egyptian squadrons were based there: Sukhoi Su-7s, MiG-19s and MiG-21s. According to the standards of those days, these were very advanced aircraft against which our Mysteres were at a disadvantage.

Our foursome is among the first to take off. My Numbers Two and Four are young, almost totally inexperienced pilots. We fly so low that we leave wakes of foam on the sea. Strict radio silence adds to the tension. Everyone is deep in his own thoughts. Suddenly I see Number Four going up and down, up and down. My heart skips a beat. I'm worried about him; we're so low he could hit the water. I can't break radio silence to warn him – I have to be satisfied with annoyed glances in his direction. I look again, and now there's only one aircraft on my right. We've started off on the wrong foot. One plane gone!

We fly on. We reach Bardiwal, but not from the right direction, and now I'm under a lot of pressure. We fly deeper into Sinai and discover low stratus clouds blotting out the sky; these will get in the way. According to the original plan, we're supposed to climb in order to bear in on the field and drop our bombs. Because of the clouds we won't be able to see the targets. God's not with us today. I know that if the attack fails, everything will be lost. And then we'll really be able to talk about the last one to leave turning out the lights.

We cross the Canal, and patches of sky appear between the clouds. Here and there you can see through them. Then, just before Fayid, the visibility clears. We go in to attack.

Coming out of my bombing run I see four MiGs ready to scramble. I release my ordnance, and two of them immediately catch fire.

As I start setting up to get my formation back together, a giant Antonov-12 materializes before me, coming in to land head-on. A pleasure. I'll be able to return to base with a sure kill! I radio the formation of my plans, bring my sights up on him, fire – and nothing happens. A malfunction! I swear quietly and leave the Antonov. On the way back we strafe a ground emplacement; all together our mission score is sixteen MiGs.

The whole way home we see smoke rising from the airfields that have been hit. On landing it turns out that Number Four was not lost; he returned to Hatzerim because of a malfunction. So the mission has been a success. The only frustration is the Antonov I missed.

A few years after the war the memoirs of Mohammed Hassanein Heikal were published, and I learned that inside the Antonov, which only fate had prevented from being shot down, had been General Amar, the Egyptian Chief of Staff, and all his generals. They had been on an inspection flight in Sinai and were finishing up with a landing at Fayid. According to Heikal, the Antonov pilot received about seventeen commendations for his brilliant evasion of the missiles the Israeli aircraft fired at him.

Chapter 5
THEY WON'T FIGHT ANYMORE

During the Six Day War Brigadier General (Res) Ran Pecker was a Mirage squadron commander. On the first day of the war he led three attack sorties against Egyptian airfields.

Just five minutes stood between failure and success, and in my bones I felt the war would turn out differently if I didn't make up for the delay. Five minutes on which everything depended: a mission on behalf of the nation, the squadron's honour, long years of training, and personal prestige as a squadron commander and senior flight leader. It was merely an administrative mistake, but because of it we took off for Inshas five minutes late, and if I didn't make up the time ... it was better not to think about it. Better to run on, squeezing the maximum performance out of the aircraft and ignoring the pressure and everything else happening around me. As long as they didn't call us back. If we could just arrive on time. Five cursed minutes that could send everything down the drain.

The evening before everything had looked like a sure thing, a real formula for success: a squadron proud and unified; the best of warriors, most of them with a wealth of experience, steeped in fighting spirit, self-assured, and convinced of victory. The base commander had called the squadron leaders and told us the war we had been preparing so much for in the previous weeks would begin the next day. I told my pilots to go home, get some sleep, and gather their

31

strength. No one listened; they stayed at the squadron. I went around to the technicians, to the revetments. I looked the aircraft over; everything was perfect. The only thing left was to wait for zero-hour.

In the first attack wave I was slated to lead a formation of four Mirages to Inshas, a top-rate Egyptian airfield on the outskirts of Cairo, and the home of forty-two MiG-21s kept on immediate intercept status. Their job was to protect Cairo, the delta and the nearby airfields. It was top priority to put Inshas out of action before the fighting broke out; if its MiGs were allowed to take off, the element of surprise would be lost. The damage they might inflict on our attacking forces could be significant, and our Ouragans and Mysteres could find themselves up against the superior MiG-21s. On the ground it would be possible to destroy forty-two aircraft; in the air it would be much more complicated. If they launched their interceptors, the outcome of the whole war might be altered. As long as we got to Inshas on time ... As long as they didn't get to take off ...

All the checks had been carried out; the formation was ready to go. Other aircraft were taking off, joining up into organized formations in the air. My foursome was waiting patiently; we still had plenty of time until take-off. Suddenly I saw a formation of Vautours – which were supposed to take off after us – heading into the air. Just to be sure I leafed through the schedule – and the mix-up hit me like lightning: we were five minutes late! Someone had made a mistake with the computations. I was flooded by anxiety and shame; everyone was already in the air, and I, the one who had to get to target first, was still on the ground!

I headed into a hasty, intercept-style take-off and raced forward at record speed. The rest of my formation joined up along the way, not comprehending my madness. We passed between the formations of Mysteres and Ouragans, our attention primarily focused on the clock and airspeed indicator. Over the sea, off Gaza, we set up into formation and flew at 420 knots instead of the planned 360. By the time we crossed Bardawil lagoon we had made up about three minutes. We crossed the Suez Canal north of Qantara and by Faqus, about a minute before pulling into the attack, we had made up the entire delay. We arrived on time: exactly 07:45.

We pulled up, rolled, inverted and, from 6000 feet, saw Inshas field spread out before us. The MiGs stood in their ready positions, armed and with pilots in the cockpits. Not one of them scrambled. On our first pass we released our bombs one-third and two-thirds down the runway, putting it out of action. Then we dropped down low and began to strafe.

At the briefing the instructions had been: 'Up to three strafing passes, according to the amount of anti-aircraft fire and what the flight leader thinks.' It was thought that they definitely would open up with ack-ack, and that was the limit on the number of passes. But I felt this would be a historic, one-time opportunity, and decided to keep on attacking until the next formation arrived and we heard the Super Mysteres coming in over the field.

We made five long, low strafing passes. The MiGs had a gasoline tank in the fuselage used for the main engine starter. When these tanks were hit the explosion set the aircraft on fire. Dozens of planes caught fire and burned on the apron near the runway, some with the pilots inside – the same pilots who were on top alert.

The anti-aircraft fire increased. We heard the Super Mysteres pulling up to come in, and we departed to the northeast. A glance to right and left, and a feeling of relief: my foursome was complete and everyone was in place. Shlomo, Lizik and Asher – wonderful pilots and true warriors.

We flew away from the field; a last glance to the rear, where black smoke was rising. Everything was burning, and a feeling of satisfaction coursed through the veins. On the way home we strafed targets of opportunity, and columns of smoke rose from all the fields along the way. We knew we had won the war; we had surprised them and beaten them.

The next target was Abu Suweir, an airfield in the delta packed with planes. After that came Hurghada and the last mission – Cairo International airport. We'd not planned on hitting this field; there was supposedly a gentlemen's agreement that warplanes would not take off from there, and our fighters would not attack. Later it turned out the Egyptians had not got the message and they began massing at Cairo International surviving aircraft from the bases which had been destroyed. Dozens of operational aircraft were gathered there and it was decided to attack them.

As I said, between raids on Abu Suweir and Cairo we attacked Hurghada – a distant and isolated airfield on the edge of the desert southwest of Sharm e-Sheikh. The initial plan had been to take care of bases posing an immediate danger, but by afternoon it was decided to hit the more distant ones as well.

We took off for Hurghada as a foursome. Until Sharm we flew at 30,000 feet, loaded with maximum fuel and weapons – bombs and cannons. Near Sharm we dropped to low altitude, almost on the surface of the Red Sea and, at the designated spot, we turned 90 degrees west, increased speed to 500 knots, and climbed along the plateau to Hurghada. Everything was quiet and reassuring. But with our pull-up for the attack the picture changed; the moment I lifted my nose for the bombing run the ack-ack turned deadly.

At this point I want to interrupt the flow of events to deal with the subject of 'deadly ack-ack'. In all my years with the Air Force I have heard many pilots talk of 'deadly' anti-aircraft fire. I don't always agree with them; everything, of course, being relative. On just two of the four hundred or so operational flights that I logged was I caught by really deadly anti-aircraft fire. The first was at Hurghada; that was hellish. For about five minutes they fired all kinds, from whatever was handy, non-stop and at a tremendous rate.

We were over completely open terrain. There were no trees, no buildings, nothing to hide behind or put between ourselves and the fire. The gun crews were in direct visual contact with us. There's no doubt they were waiting for us to show up; Hurghada's defenders had already heard of the strikes against other airfields and were wound tight as a spring. They probably felt like the bride at a wedding: she knows she's going to get it, she just doesn't know when.

We had no choice but to fly right into it. And there at Hurghada we showed the results of the precise preparations before the war at Tel Nof; we worked exactly as we did during practice, and this is the greatest compliment one can give a squadron.

We knew we were 1000 kilometres from home and had to give our all and be the best, because there was no other way. We knew that if we didn't do this someone else would have to go back there and do it instead.

We made one bombing pass and three strafing runs, ignoring the ack-ack. The runway was hit and gaping craters opened up. Planes and helicopters were smashed on the tarmac and left burning. At the end of the second pass one of my pilots – Rubik Rosen, a boy who was a stickler for precision and brave as the devil – informed me he was low on fuel. I made an unusual decision and told him to return to base by himself. I knew there were no active enemy bases between us and home, and I planned to catch up with him. It was simply a shame to break off the attack in the middle.

We made another circuit and I heard Bukie, a young pilot from Kfar Haim, shouting at me in a high soprano 'Break! A MiG's sitting on you!' I looked back and saw a MiG-19 sitting close in, about 300 metres away. Bukie's yell over the radio made me do something to get things back on the correct footing. In the quietest tone possible I answered, 'Say again.' He hesitated for a split second, then repeated his message in a completely different, relatively relaxed voice. I felt we were now on the right track, although our situation was bad: three Mirages, low on fuel and ammunition, far from home and fighting against four fresh MiGs above their home base.

I pulled a trick on the MiG called Let Him Pass, and shot him down over the field. I looked up to the right and saw that A was sandwiched between two MiGs. I went after the second one and told A to stay on the one in front. After about half a minute he informed me that he had shot down the MiG. A few seconds later I shot down mine. During this whole time the guns continued to fire at us, at them, at everyone, without being choosy. I sent A home and looked for Bukie. He said he was sitting on a MiG. He was still talking when I caught sight of a shocking drama; a MiG-19 was coming in for a landing, his landing gear and flaps down. He was flying at 180 knots, followed by a desperately twisting Mirage that was trying to hold him in its sights – all of this in a glut of anti-aircraft fire that didn't let up for a moment. I shouted to Bukie, 'Break right! Leave the MiG! Unload! Gain speed!' He broke and the MiG touched down, hit a crater and broke into pieces. I threw a last glance at Hurghada and we left the field behind.

We returned home from a long-distance attack, after mixing it in a dogfight and downing four MiGs. Thousands of Egyptian officers and soldiers – who had known they were protected by anti-aircraft guns, and especially by four pilots from the base, and who afterwards witnessed the raid and the air battle – wouldn't be fighting anymore. Every time they had to do battle the drama of Hurghada would appear before their eyes.

Chapter 6
FIVE MIGs IN THREE DAYS

Brigadier General Giora Rom, then a Mirage pilot, missed out on the first attack during the Six Day War. At nine in the morning of 5 June he shot down his first MiG. Before the war was over he had tallied five enemy aircraft.

I started the Six Day War feeling like a wallflower. I wasn't assigned to any of the great strikes against Arab airfields: instead I remained behind on air defence alert. Not until the whole base took off in front of my eyes did I believe war would break out. It's difficult to digest the fact that tomorrow, or the next day, there will be a war. The first, overwhelming reaction is not to believe it. And when I sat on the squadron's intercept stand I still didn't believe it would be anything serious. Only when the aircraft began to take off, and I was sitting in a plane doing nothing, was I overcome by a terrible frustration. I decided that this was it, the beginning of a war, and I was out of business. This frustration grew immensely when the aircraft returned from the attack and I was still on the ground.

At nine in the morning someone heard my prayers and I was scrambled on an attack. The objective was Abu Suweir airfield near Ismailia in Egypt. This was my first mission beyond the border; I was a Mirage pilot, a twenty-two-year-old lieutenant, among the youngest in the squadron.

We had little fuel because we were originally earmarked

for local air defence. We gained altitude and headed toward Egypt; arriving over the field we saw it had already been taken care of: the runways had already been bombed, and on them a number of Il-28 bombers were burning. To the side stood a MiG-21, which suddenly taxied to the parallel runway and took off. I descended and came in on him in firing position. My leader immediately stopped me. 'Don't touch him. I'll shoot him down.' In those days I still had some discipline. I moved aside; my leader closed in and brought him down. This was the first time I saw an airplane explode in mid-air.

And then, almost as if it had been planned this way, the door to hell opened up. The skies were suddenly filled with aircraft, and there were dogfights and a whole insanity of explosions, flashes of fire and mushrooms of smoke. And I, you mustn't forget, was a greenhorn among greenhorns.

I noticed two MiG-21s chasing our Mirages. I went onto afterburner, locked in on one of the MiGs, and came into range. I fired at 200 metres but didn't hit him. It was a terrible moment; all my self-confidence was dashed to the ground. My heart pounded to the rhythm of only one thought: here I am, having prepared three years for this fight – and I missed him. I tried a second time. I closed in to 150 metres, fired – and he blew up in front of my eyes. Now I didn't care if we lost the war.

I returned to the airfield, picked up on another MiG-21, chased after him, fired my cannons – and he went down. I was drunk with victory. I went back to the field once more and saw another MiG-21 in the distance. I fired while still far away and didn't see whether he was hit. However I was short of fuel, below the minimum, and decided to squelch my enthusiasm.

I descended to a very low altitude and began flying home. On the way my leader informed me that he was bailing out because he was out of fuel. I went easier on the fuel and made it back to base. I was euphoric; two aerial victories, my fuel had held out, and everything had gone smoothly. In my eyes this was a great victory.

In the afternoon I was to attack the international airport at Cairo. I was already in the cockpit when the squadron driver brought me a note and a map. They had switched targets; we ended up being sent to H-4, a distant field in Syria, close to

Tadmor, the Syrian security prison. It was hard not to think about this.

We went out as a foursome: Eitan Carni, who led, Asher Snir, Eliezer Prigat, and me. The flight was very long, about half an hour each way. We arrived at the objective and, before the attack, saw two MiG-21s cruising near the field. In those days we had different norms; orders to adhere to the game-plan were so stringent that the problem was how to attack while holding off from shooting the MiGs down.

We hit the field, and Asher Snir hurried off to shoot down one of the MiGs. We took turns strafing the field; coming out from one of my attacks I saw a MiG-21 about 1000 metres from Prigat. I gave him a warning, and then began calculating how to down the MiG before anyone else could. I released my drop tanks, turned in towards him, and we began to slug it out. And then something unusual happened: three more Mirages arrived over the field. One of them took a shot at the MiG, only to suffer a compressor stall. The MiG turned its attention from me and toward the stricken Mirage. I clung to the MiG, hearing in the background the Mirage pilot shouting for help over the radio. The MiG fired two missiles at the Mirage, but they didn't hit. I aimed and fired; the MiG caught fire right above the field and began spinning down.

I had been left by myself. I climbed to 35,000 feet and crossed all of Syria, alone. I had little fuel left. On the long flight back I thought of just one thing – the Sea of Galilee. At the Sea of Galilee the whole world changes, and every time you're above it you have the same, comfortable feeling; you've made it. This time, too, I made it back in one piece.

The next day I led a formation on an attack on the Golan Heights. We went to hit an emplacement on the road leading up from the B'not Ya'akov Bridge to the Upper Customs House, where there's now a large monument to the Armoured Corps. The whole Hula Valley was on fire, and from the air everything looked like one great cloud of smoke. We bombed from high altitude, then came down to strafe enemy tanks. We were caught by very heavy anti-aircraft fire.

On the third pass I felt a tremendous smack under the seat. The first thought to flash through my mind was: so this is what Angel felt. Danny Angel was a good friend of mine who was killed on the first day of the war.

I looked around the cockpit and saw no warning lights.

Everything was dead. I turned right to cross the Jordan. It was clear that I was heading for a bail-out. My engine gauge showed 10,000 rpm; until then I had thought 8700 rpm was the point where an engine flies apart. The turbine was indeed on its way towards coming apart, but I kept going. I had no electrical power in the cockpit. The control column was stiff, and I began to fly with two hands; the stick was constantly pulling me forward. I tried to climb, but nothing worked. It turned out that a 37mm shell had struck the aircraft right below my seat. The whole left side of the cockpit had been affected, including the instrument junction box and the control column rods. Shell splinters had penetrated my leg, and it had been bleeding the whole time.

I headed towards Ramat David, and found myself above the field, ready to land, without any instruments. I lowered my gear with the emergency system but, since the green lights would not go on, I didn't know if the wheels had indeed gone down. I banked towards the sun to see my shadow, but this gave no indication of whether the gear was locked. I couldn't line up on the runway without controls and with an aircraft that was giving me only a quarter of its normal performance. I flew towards Tivon, made a very wide turn to straighen up in line with the runway. I descended, gripping the stiff control column with both hands, and came down right on the runway. I stopped the aircraft and tried to rise from my seat, but couldn't.

I spend that night at Afula hospital, not forgiving myself for missing the war. In the morning I phoned the base, said I had been released from the hospital and asked one of the men to sneak me some coveralls, a G-suit and new boots. I then went to the hospital gate in a wheelchair and waited for the base transport. When I got to the squadron, I put on the coveralls, and went down to Operations. Everyone was aghast. The commander of the base forbade me to fly without the doctor's okay, but the doctor didn't have a chance; he gave me permission without any argument.

They had assigned me to the squadron's last flight for the day. We went out in the afternoon as a threesome to hit an Egyptian armoured brigade on the road between Ras Sudr and Sharm e-Sheikh. On the way, ground control instructed us to dump our bombs and head north at 20,000 feet. Near the ground I noticed the flicker of a MiG, which I immediately lost. I released my drop tanks, lowered my nose and dove, telling the others to follow. I came down very low and saw two MiG-17s battling two of our Super Mysteres. I went towards the dogfight and turned over, in time to see one of our planes going into the ground.

The MiGs flew very low and began to run. I gave chase, leaving behind the other two aircraft in my formation. They started shouting, 'Where are you?' I said I was chasing the MiGs eastwards. My true direction was west, but I wanted the victories for myself.

I was alone with the MiGs. I closed in and fired at the one at the back. Pieces flew off. He raised his nose and started to climb. The other MiG fled. I went in close to the stricken aircraft and saw that the warning lights were on in the cockpit, the canopy was gone, and there was no pilot. He had ejected. The MiG dove into the ground north of Bir Gafgafa.

I lowered my nose and began to chase the MiG that had run. I flew very low so I'd be able to see him above the horizon. It was sunset and the sun was quite blinding, but I found the MiG above the swamps near Ismailia and we began to mix it over the Canal. He fought very hard, breaking and turning when he had to and trying to get me out in front. Then my leader called me and ordered me to leave everything and return home. His instructions were accompanied by the reasoning that 'you don't fight alone'. I stayed for another half a minute, shot down the MiG, and returned by myself.

Despite the satisfaction of the double victory, it was no longer euphoria. The atmosphere at the base on the third day of the war put a damper on the desire to celebrate. Our attention was centred more on our losses than our victories. I landed, drained from the effort and the exhaustion, and went to the mess hall. The sergeant major refused me supper because I was late. Things were back to normal.

Chapter 7
UNPLANNED OBJECTIVES

The activities of the Air Force spread to all the fronts during the Six Day War. The story of Brigadier General (Res) Aharon 'Yallo' Shavit, which opens this chapter, is about a sortie to Syria. Brigadier General B carried out a long range mission to Iraq, and Colonel (Res) Uri Even-Nir participated in the sole air battle against the Lebanese Air Force.

Brig Gen (Res) Yallo Shavit In 1967, I commanded a squadron of Super Mysteres. It was a very nice aircraft, but no king of the skies. Most experts considered the MiG-21, which it had to go up against, to be much superior, very powerful and more manoeuvrable. There were many who feared a confrontation between the MiG-21 and the Super Mystere. But in the squadron we were sure that our aircraft, with pilots operating them properly, could take on the MiG. We worked hard at it and I think we were ready as we went into the Six Day War.

On the first day of the war – my third or fourth sortie of the day – we were sent in a foursome to attack Sayqal, a large Syrian airfield on the edge of the Syrian-Iraqi desert. My Numbers Two and Four were young fellows with little experience of frontline aircraft.

We took a heading almost straight to Sayqal, and were crossing the West Bank near Nablus when Number Three informed me that he had been hit. I looked over and saw a small fuel leak from his right wing tank. Okay, what do we do? Sayqal was a long way off and we needed every drop of fuel. I told him to continue for the time being, but to monitor his fuel carefully. Below a certain minimum he was to return home, but he must remember that we were at war, and if the problem wasn't serious he was to continue.

We crossed the Jordan, passed the southern Golan Heights, and arrived at the Laja. It was difficult navigating over the monotonous Laja Desert, so we relied on the tall pillars of smoke already rising from fields that had been attacked – Dumeir and Damascus International in Syria, Mafraq and Amman in Jordan (Sayqal had not yet been hit, but another quartet was on its way a few minutes ahead of us). Good; we were running in the right direction and were on time. In those days there were no sophisticated navigation aids like there are today. Just a clock, a map and a compass. That was it.

Approaching Sayqal, the leader of the formation ahead of me said, 'We've hit the runway. Be careful, there are MiG-21s defending ...' Smoke had begun to rise on the horizon ahead of us, and this solved the problem of navigating the last leg.

I heard the part about the MiGs and ordered my formation to climb immediately to 6000 feet. A Super Mystere needs a lot of energy to go up against a MiG, and height is energy. I checked Number Three's fuel situation; it was still reasonable, so I told him to make one bombing pass, then climb to altitude and wait for us: he didn't have enough fuel to mix it with MiGs, but it would be dangerous to return home alone.

We arrived over the field and, looking around, I didn't see any MiGs in the air. The formation that had already attacked was gone; Sayqal was now spread out before us, just waiting for the bombs that were to fall. Well, if there were no MiGs around, there would be no problems.

We went in to the attack; a few seconds to aim and the bombs were hitting the runway. I pulled out to the left, looked back and saw my formation was now too large. I counted: one, two, three, four – and five and six. This meant two MiGs were already sitting behind us and closing in. I ordered Number Three to break right, as opposed to the rest of us, and to try and avoid a fight. That left three, two of whom were kids with just four months' experience in frontline aircraft. The MiGs were straight on our six o'clock, a classic situation to contend with.

I told Number Four to start evading and Number Two to try and get the MiG on Four's tail into a sandwich. I began to close on the MiG at the back, but the bastard saw me and immediately pulled up 90 degrees. Clearly I'd have no chance if I went after him; this was exactly where the MiG had the advantage. In addition, we didn't have enough fuel to wage a long fight over Sayqal.

I decided to tempt the MiG pilot. He had pulled up, so I lowered my nose and showed him my belly, as if I were making a getaway. Now he turned into a hero and lowered his own nose. I manoeuvred and caught him from above. We dropped down low: 2000 feet, then 1000 feet. He pulled into a tight turn above the base, where they were firing at both of us from every rooftop and hangar. A real party.

Evidently, the MiG was superior and I wasn't holding him. I changed direction; he fell for it and reversed. Here's where I caught him. One more reverse of bank, a relatively long ripple of fire, and the MiG crashed in the middle of the field, right among the hangars.

At this point I was down to 160 knots – an amusing speed when you're over an enemy airfield. I increased speed and heard Number Three call out: 'One, good for you!' Him, sitting up in the bleachers, watching the battle and giving our grades! 'Okay, and what about Two and Four?' I asked. And then we began hearing all kinds of shouting over the radio. 'I see him! Now I don't!' And suddenly I heard my Number Two: 'The MiG's in front of me. What do I do now?'

I shouted at him, 'Press the trigger, idiot!'

After a second of silence he came back and said, 'Wow, a wing's flown off.' A pilot with the mentality of a cadet, but already shooting down MiGs over Sayqal.

That's it. We strafed a bit till we ran low on fuel, then climbed and flew home.

Brig Gen B One of the missions assigned us on the second day of the war was an attack on the Iraqi H-3 airfield. Why Iraq? Well, the war started against Egypt and Syria, and afterwards Jordan. But at a later stage it spread to other objectives that weren't planned at the beginning. Iraq's involvement began with an attack by a Tupolev bomber against the Abic factory near Netanya. Our reaction was to send a formation of Vautours, to strike at H-3 on the same day. The formation met intense opposition from Iraqi Hunters and MiG-21s; because the first raid failed it was decided to hit the field again.

This time it was planned to send a quartet of Vautours escorted by a pair of Mirages. Other than an estimate as to location, we had no maps or intelligence data on the field. It was decided to cross the border at the southern edge of the Sea of Galilee, and from there fly along the oil pipeline to our objective. I was to be Number Four. We were to fly at low altitude with the Mirages at the back; as we bombed the field, they would fend off the aircraft scrambled against us.

We left early in the morning. My aircraft was already standing outside the hangar. I made the usual pre-flight walkaround and began to go up the ladder. As I planted my foot on the first rung I noticed a large shiny aircraft, without camouflage, arriving from the east at an altitude of about a 1000 feet. At first glance it looked like a Boeing, but a second look confirmed my suspicions: it was a Tupolev Tu-16, obviously coming to bomb our airfield.

I asked the mechanics if they knew the aircraft approaching. 'Of course,' they answered, 'it's a Boeing.'

'No,' I said, 'it's a Tupolev.'

In an instant they had fled for shelter. At that point the siren went off, and anti-aircraft fire opened up from all directions. The Tupolev began a righthand turn and the rear gunner fired on the base. From somewhere above, a Mirage surprised the bomber with a missile; the aircraft crashed to the ground.

It turned out that the Tupolev had come from the same field we were going to attack. A small world.

We got into our aircraft, strapped in, started up and took off, with the Mirages following. We flew low towards the target; across the Jordanian–Iraqi border we discovered a great laager of an Iraqi brigade, which was organizing to join the war. Gritting our teeth, we flew on.

We turned along the road leading to H-3. Clouds of dust rose from the H-3 runways as a pair of Mig-21s scrambled towards us; the dust gave away their location. Our Mirages headed for them as we pulled to the east to make our bombing run from left of the runway. Entering our bombing pass we discovered a Hunter ready to land. Number One released his bombs on the runway and the Hunter rolled wide of the strip, on fire. Number Two went in next; coming out of his run there was another Hunter, which had been on its way to land, but was now going after Number One.

'One, a Hunter's coming in on you!' we all shouted over the radio. He broke hard to the left, while Number Two tried to fire at the Hunter. No go. Number Two dropped out of the turn; Number Three came out of his bombing run in good position and was able to set himself up a little better on the Hunter.

'I've downed him, I've downed him!' he shouted. It was a very encouraging thing to hear amid the shower of fire. Then it was my turn. I made my pass, and noted that I had enough bombs left for another run. Pulling up I discovered a Hunter in the downwind leg, with his wheels and flaps down and on his way to land.

I was happy for the opportunity and planned to knock him down. I switched my sights to air–air and closed in at high speed, but he was apparently warned by the tower and suddenly broke left at low altitude, getting out of the circuit just before I could open fire. I gave up any thoughts of chasing him; I wouldn't be able to make the necessary manoeuvres with all the ordnance I was carrying.

I straightened out and set up for my second bombing run. An anti-aircraft battery at the end of the runway opened up on me with concentrated fire. The suddenness of the whole thing made me straighten out, exposing myself to the gunners. Of course this was absolute stupidity, and a split second later I recovered and went in on my bombing run, using my cannons against the ack-ack battery.

Coming out I made another run and strafed a line of aircraft in the middle of the runway. Receiving instructions to break contact and head west, I joined formation along with the Mirages, which had come in from the north; they left a MiG-21 on fire and on its way to the ground.

We broke off to the west, and on the way home paid a debt: coming in over the Iraqi brigade laager, we strafed it. We then crossed the border back into our own territory, completely out of ammunition.

Aside from carrying out our mission, we achieved an additional effect: from this point on Iraq's involvement in the war would be reduced to almost zero.

Col (Res) Uri Even-Nir It began on the second day of the Six Day War. I was a lad of twenty-seven, deputy commander of a Mirage squadron at Ramat David. My aircraft was on the apron by the runway and I was inside – strapped in, relaxing, listening to the radio and awaiting instructions. Suddenly, three Hunters flashed between the eucalyptus trees beyond the taxiway. They came into view, inverted, and pulled in to the attack. What can I say except that this was one of the shittiest feelings. Here I was, sitting in an aircraft, totally exposed and an attractive target; a split second separated me from becoming trapped. I shouted over the radio that aircraft were attacking the field, then scrambled and bounced around behind another three Mirages.

We split into pairs and began to search the valley for the Hunters. The other pair turned towards Beit Shean, while we turned north. We didn't find a thing, as if the ground had swallowed them up. Later we learned the Hunters had attacked the chicken coops at Nahalal, this being the first thing that flashed in front of their eyes.

Meanwhile we were told to patrol the northern Sea of Galilee. Back and forth, back and forth. Then came instructions from ground control: 'Target in the north, green light.' We raced towards the objective as the controller continued to update: 'Target at 20,000 feet. Unclear whether one aircraft or two.' As we approached the border the controller informed us that the aircraft had left Israeli airspace. We turned south. Two minutes later the message changed: 'He's turning again. Head north.' We went into pursuit but the controller cut us off: 'He's heading out. Turn south.' Things went this way three times. The third time I couldn't stand it and asked permission to hit him and put an end to this game.

We released our drop tanks and ran after the bogey. Accelerating, we crossed the border into Lebanon and closed range. At seven miles I made visual contact and identified the target immediately. It was a single Hunter, flying like an idiot at 20,000 feet, heading north. I looked around. The skies were completely clear.

The Hunter was flying slowly, loaded down with rockets and drop tanks. I throttled back and deployed my air brakes, but still slipped out from behind him. My speed was too high. I started a barrel roll around him to figure out a way of getting in to the required range. During the roll I passed near the Hunter's cockpit. We were really head to head. The pilot looked me straight in the eye – and did nothing.

I slipped back, settled down about 250 metres behind, and began to fire my cannons. This had no effect on him; he continued to fly straight and did nothing to get himself out of this predicament. I fired another burst. Pieces flew off his aircraft, but he continued to fly straight. Another burst – and the thing flew on! Every burst that I fired hit him. Another burst, and more pieces would fly off. But, in his own little world, the Hunter pilot continued to fly straight and slow. His fuel began leaking but he still flew. I remember telling my Number Two that this was like plucking a chicken.

I started getting impatient. I closed in to 150 metres and decided to hit him with another burst, not letting go until he blew up. I fired, and a huge piece of metal suddenly separated from the Hunter, soared in my direction and struck my left air intake. I suffered a compressor stall and my engine stopped pulling. I moved aside and told Number Two, 'I'm in trouble. Finish him off.' I was still speaking as the Hunter's ejection seat flew out – the pilot was calling it quits. He was getting out, and I was in trouble.

We were at 15,000 feet above Riyaq airfield, east of Beirut, a place not highly recommended for a problem like this. I tried to open the throttle a little, but right away noticed another compressor stall. It was clear I would have to eject.

We headed towards the sea, with Number Two running around me like a sheepdog, making sure I was still going and calling for rescue boats in case I should have to bail out over the water. Over the radio they were pounding away with instructions: 'Try this, try that,' and I was still flying. I don't know how, but we made it back to base. When we opened up the engine we couldn't believe our eyes. It was completely shattered, the turbine blades were destroyed – and despite everything the engine had kept working.

Later we found out that because of the downing of the Hunter, the Lebanese decided that this was both their opening and closing action of the Six Day War. From this point on, they pointed to me and said, 'That's the one who, with his first victory, routed the whole Lebanese army.'

Chapter 8
PLUCKED FROM THE THROAT OF
THE LION

Major General (Res) David Ivri, former commander of the IAF, provided air cover for a pilot who had bailed out over Syria on the last day of the Six Day War, until the pilot was rescued.

The mission was an air strike on the Golan Heights during the morning hours of Saturday, 11 June 1967, the last day of the Six Day War. The Air Force was concentrating almost all its activity against the Syrians, with just a few flights allocated to other objectives. The sortie rate had slowed down and the number of missions was reduced; the Egyptians and Jordanians had been removed from the picture and we had gained absolute air superiority over the Syrians.

Just a few weeks had passed since I was appointed commander of the Air Force Flight Academy. Before that I had led a Mirage squadron at Ramat David, and I still had a deep emotional attachment to that unit. But during the war I was posted to a different Mirage squadron as a flight leader and duty commander, and the war saw me putting down roots fast in this squadron, in terms of responsibility and authority. I began to feel like a full member, not just an observer in the gallery. Five days of fighting with the new squadron made me feel at home, and for some reason it quickly distanced me from my previous unit. Here the meaning of war became clear; I learned that experiences shared in war can overshadow all existing relationships. War

49

creates a powerful and emotional bond between warriors. One facet of this bond rests in the concept of 'comrades in arms', and this, essentially, was the core of this sortie.

My partner for the attack was G, a junior Mirage pilot who had transferred to the Air Force from the paratroopers. We ended up flying a number of sorties together during the war and during the alert which preceded it. He really impressed me; he was a pilot steeped in confidence, and one could trust him and count on him. He later commanded the Mirage squadron I had led, and logged many operational sorties and aerial victories.

The aircraft were armed with two 500 kilogram bombs and two 30mm cannons. We strapped ourselves in, turned on the radio, and waited for instructions to go. In order not to lose our place in the line of aircraft ready to roll we reminded the controllers of our existence every few minutes over the radio. It was unnecessary, of course, but it made us feel better.

Time passed and it was almost noon; it started to be annoying, sitting for so long. I had the sudden feeling they'd start feeling very sorry for us and would shortly rotate us, and that a minute later there'd be an order to scramble. We would then have paid the price for the tiring wait while our relief, without having paid their dues, would get the hoped-for scramble.

Finally, the instructions to go. Adrenaline accelerates through the blood. The mechanics go into action. The revs build up; throttle completely back and the engine catches. The checklist is automatic, hands flashing about the cockpit, and the aircraft responds as if reacting to my excitement. The Mirage has a soul; this is not merely an airplane.

In the air we hear that a formation from a neighbouring Mirage squadron has been sent ahead of us on the same mission. Our turn will come when they finish. The route cuts across Samaria, exactly above Nablus, an area we had been forbidden to fly over just a few days ago. Our intention is to cross the Jordan River south of the Sea of Galilee and reach the Golan Heights from the south, not west, in order to allow freedom of action on the front lines.

We listen in on the formation ahead of us, and near Nablus it becomes evident that something's happened. The leader calls his Number Two but gets no answer. We all go to radio silence so that any answer won't be missed. A little while later the leader announces in a high-pitched and trembling voice that his Number Two's plane is on fire, and he's apparently ejected. We wait in silence till he says that he sees a parachute.

We're already southwest of the Sea of Galilee and G announces that he sees the parachute. I tell him to maintain visual contact and lead me in that direction till I see the 'chute for myself. I've already been told that G has the eyes of an eagle and can pick out aircraft beyond the usual range. And here the boy has proved it; from fifteen kilometres, and at a downward angle, he finds the parachute. I locate it only after we've closed to three or four kilometres.

The other flight leader is relieved to hear these developments. His fuel is running out and we agree to take responsibility for rescuing the pilot. From the altitude at which the pilot bailed out it will take some five minutes until he reaches the ground. As a matter of fact, we're over the area before he comes in. While waiting for the pilot to finish his descent we hear his leader talking with ground control; he sounds more troubled than he should normally be and hints that the pilot who ejected is not from the rank and file. (It later turned out the pilot was Colonel S, the base commander.)

As the parachute comes close to the ground, it becomes apparent that touch-down will be near Shekh Miskin, close to Syrian troop concentrations. We notice flashes of fire, but don't know if it's aimed at us or the pilot. We go in to attack the Syrians in order to keep up the continuity of fire against the area. I inform G that we'll make individual passes, putting down a minimum of fire each time and trying to save fuel to allow us to remain over the area as long as possible. We drop to 500 feet and locate a BTR armoured vehicle with many other vehicles by the side of the road. They open fire, and this is the sign for us to start bombing.

Out of the corner of my eye, while coming out of the first pass, I see the downed pilot jumping from boulder to boulder at the peak of a rocky knoll. (We later found out he had broken an arm and a leg, but despite this he scurried about like a gazelle.) The knoll is a kilometre from the road along which Syrian troops are now gathering, and it's clear that this is going to be a race against the clock. When will the rescue helicopter show up? Will we run out of ammunition? Will there be enough fuel to keep watch over the downed pilot? When will the Syrians make their move?

G understands all the potential problems, as do I, and our co-ordination is excellent. We loose continuous fire in small amounts against the Syrians, who have spread out. At this stage we're efficient enough to suppress their fire, as well as their desire to move towards the knoll where S, alone and helpless, is hiding among the boulders. We complete our bombing passes and switch to strafing with our guns in small, decisive bursts.

Over the radio we hear that the helicopter is on its way. We pass on instructions and information, hoping to guide it directly to S. And here G's eagle eyes strike again; he locates the helicopter while it's still far off and directs it to the knoll as I continue to strafe. To save ammunition I hold my fire on every other pass; right now I have to save some ammunition for the critical part, when the helicopter lands and the Syrians increase their fire.

The helicopter's progress seems appallingly slow, and I have a strange urge to spur him on over the radio. But I hold my tongue.

Meanwhile I check the fuel situation with G; he has 300 litres less than me – in fact he has the minimum fuel needed for a normal return to base. He says he thinks he has a fuel leak (this was indeed the case; he had been hit in a wing tank by small arms fire, which caused a small but continuous leak). I make a quick calculation: he should go home, but the situation in the field calls for him to stay. A moment of indecision, and we agree that he'll remain until the end of the critical phase; when the rescue helicopter takes off he'll leave and land at Ramat David.

The helicopter comes in for a landing and Syrian fire increases, aimed directly at the knoll. Either they've got used to our presence and are now bolder, or it's the helicopter's presence that's egging them on. At any rate we increase our strafing runs. The helicopter lands and I make a low pass, close to the landing site, and fire my last shell. My ammunition is spent, G is also out, and he informs me he has 250 litres of fuel. With this amount it's almost impossible to return to a circuit. We take leave of one another; he flies to Ramat David and I remain with the helicopter. I ask ground control to keep an eye on him, to guide him directly to base and give him landing priority. Deep down I feel G will be fine.

My own fuel guage shows about 600 litres and I decide to make another dummy strafing pass to keep the fire off the helicopter. It's the only weapon I have left after having used up my ammunition. In the middle of my run I notice the helicopter drawing near the Syrians without seeing them. I warn the pilot over the radio and he moves away.

The helicopter heads towards our own lines at a speed that looks like a crawl, and the chopper commander announces that the rescued pilot is indeed wounded, but that he's all right. The fuel in my tanks is dropping and I have to leave; a pair of Super Mysteres takes over escorting the helicopter. On my way home I hear its pilot announce that he's entering our territory, and I'm filled with relief.

I request word on G. He hasn't let me down, having landed safely at Ramat David. I request a straight-in approach and touch down with 150 litres of fuel; this is low, but my satisfaction is complete. We have rescued a pilot in the middle of the day in an area surrounded by Syrians – and we all made it back safely, having plucked prey from the throat of a hungry lion. And who was the prey but an old friend.

Chapter 9
NO STOPS ON THE WAY

A short time after the Phantom was integrated into the Air Force ranks, eight of them were sent on the longest attack mission the IAF had ever known. The flight to Ras Banas laid the groundwork for long-range Israeli air raids ever since. Brigadier General (Res) Aharon 'Yallo' Shavit was among the Phantom pilots who took part in the bombing of the Ras Banas.

It was during the War of Attrition, on 16 May 1970. The Phantoms were still partly untried, and all of a sudden they dropped this kind of mission in our laps. Frightful. The objective was Ras Banas, way down on the Red Sea, on the border with Sudan – 450 kilometres south of Sharm e-Sheikh, a port that the Egyptian navy used as a base for a destroyer. She would come north in the Red Sea, launch commando boats with terrorists, then return to hide at the port. The straw that broke the camel's back was the sinking of the *Orit* with a sea-to-sea missile and the subsequent mining of the wreck. Our orders were to sink the destroyer. So far, so good. But it was a two-hour flight each way, and the first time the Air Force had been asked to mount a mission so deep into enemy territory.

Okay. We put together a team: eight experienced pilots and eight experienced navigators. Real lions, each one a story by himself. Zero-hour was set for four o'clock in the afternoon so we'd come out of the sun and they wouldn't be able to see us. We were fuelled to the maximum; each aircraft was equipped with three external tanks and six bombs. We were given a highly detailed briefing. Then, into the air.

We took off in battle formation: four pairs. To increase our alertness we took along bottles with special straws that could be inserted into our oxygen masks. With the liquid on the left side of the survival vest you could take as many sips as you wanted, and this would keep you alert and satisfied. By the way, this is the place to add that what they say about me isn't so: there was no whisky. I swear it!

We flew the whole way at 40,000 feet to save fuel and obviate the necessity of going low to avoid missiles, anti-aircraft fire and God knows what else. We flew straight to Sharm and turned south along the middle of the Red Sea. Until I flew over the Red Sea I had no idea of its width; I thought I'd see Egypt on one side and Saudi Arabia on the other. But this was no little gulf – a tremendous sea! It was a surprise for us all.

We flew for an hour and a half, two hours, before reaching the target. We maintained radio silence the whole way down, but kept visual contact. We descended before the objective, coming in at low altitude with the sun at our backs and taking them by complete surprise. We pulled up high and dove. The destroyer was there, waiting for us. It was anchored next to the jetty, carefully isolated, a grey, Soviet-built Z-class destroyer.

I was Number Six and saw the hits on the destroyer from the aircraft ahead of me. My bombs were already unnecessary, but my Number Two and I added our contributions to the festivities. All told we dropped almost fifty bombs weighing a total of twenty-four tons! When we exited the port they fired some light ack-ack; no one was hit. I glanced down and saw the destroyer going up in flames along with other vessels, among them a missile boat and a landing craft. It was a strange sight, with stains of fire floating on the water.

We left the port behind, heading out to sea at low altitude. Everyone reported his fuel situation, and all was well. We went back to 40,000 feet until we hit Israeli territory, by which time we had been flying for three hours and fifty minutes, a new record. Before this there had been no such attack mission in fighter aircraft. In today's terms, it would be something like halfway to Tunis.

The Egyptians were sure their destroyer had been beyond our reach. And after the bombing the area was completely quiet. This was a milestone in terms of ideas, planning, and perfect execution. It was a flight that led to changes in direction and opened the eyes of a lot of people. This is the way to execute missions, without heroic rescue stories after things have gone wrong. Our story would have come out if someone had ejected, had been captured, or whatnot. But the beauty of it was that everything went smoothly. We came, we bombed, we went home, and we left them with the question: How the hell did they do it?

Chapter 10
A TRUE LOSS

'It took some time until we "discovered" Shlomo Weintraub.
He graduated from Flight Academy with mediocre grades
and was no stand-out when he started on his way with the
squadron. But he had tremendous drive. He was a boy from
Kibbutz Beit Alpha with a good head on his shoulders,
thoughtful and bright. But he wasn't quite as successful with
his hands. For this reason he was initially lost among the
ranks. But by and by, thanks to his good head and stubbornness, and his refusal to give in, he became a good flier.

'I trusted him without hesitation and began to give him
chances as formation leader. Motti Hod, then commander of
the Air Force, didn't care for my initiatives; he still wasn't
sure about Weintraub. Every time Weintraub was scheduled
to lead, our squadron would be given a marginal role in the
mission. One day I decided to put an end to this "boycott"
and pleaded with Motti, "Try him once." I won Motti over,
and on the same sortie Weintraub shot down a plane. The
stigma was erased. In five months he shot down four aircraft.'
– Col (Res) Uri Even-Nir, Weintraub's squadron leader

*The story of Shlomo Weintraub's last sortie is told by Colonel
(Res) Yehuda Koren, deputy squadron leader at the time.*

On the morning of 2 February 1970 there was a scramble to
the border area with Syria. We patrolled, but there was no
contact. This was during a period of Syrian insolence, when

they tried to provoke us without let-up. They would patrol close to our lines, we would scramble towards them, and they would flee. This kind of harassment happened many times and it became clear we'd have to put a stop to it.

At the end of this futile patrol I landed and Shlomo Weintraub came up, took me aside, and told me a quartet was being organized for a special operation. 'Count me in,' he requested.

Even, the squadron leader, explained that we wanted to teach the Syrians a lesson. The plan was to maintain a high altitude patrol as bait while our four came in at low level, penetrated into Syrian air space, then came back towards the Syrian aircraft from the east. In this way we'd surprise them and catch them from two sides, keeping them from escaping.

Even was leader and Shlomo was Number Two. We took off in the afternoon in complete radio silence and flew in pairs, line astern, very fast and at very low level – less than 100 feet. Shortly after crossing, on the eastern side of the Sea of Galilee, I saw flashes coming from different places on the ground. The area was known for its heavy anti-aircraft fire. I called over the radio that there was a lot of ack-ack around, and right then I saw Weintraub's aircraft pulling up. This was against the briefing instructions and I immediately called to him, 'Two, why are you pulling?' I received no answer. I asked again. And yet again. Still silence. Even called out the same question, but the aircraft kept going up. I told Even I was pulling up after Weintraub to see what was going on. I pulled in close to Shlomo's aircraft and saw there was no canopy and no one in the cockpit. I figured he'd bailed out.

I reported the situation and we began to look for Shlomo's parachute. We found nothing. It was very strange: on the one hand there was no canopy and he could not be seen in the cockpit; on the other, I hadn't seen him parachuting to the ground. The whole time his aircraft was going up, until about 12,000 feet, when it began to drop its nose. I watched the plane dive and it was clear Shlomo was not inside. I remember I didn't even shout for him to get out because I was sure he had done long before.

The plane crashed and turned into a giant mushroom of flame. We kept circling in the hope that we'd find a sign of life from Shlomo, but we circled in vain. There was no point in going on with the mission as the Syrian had already discovered us. Their anti-aircraft fire did not let up.

Later we found out that Shlomo had been killed by a direct hit; a single shell had struck and shattered his canopy. Shlomo was killed instantly. His head was hanging down, which was why we couldn't see him in the cockpit.

Many days went by and the nagging thoughts would not let up. Why him? By the same token it could have been me. I mean, such a huge number of shells were flying by it was just rotten luck that led Shlomo to his death. The chances for a shell like that hitting him were so slim, but there was just no way to avoid it. It was not a matter of being a good or a bad pilot – bad luck lurks in every corner. There were also thoughts of what-would-have-happened-if. Maybe if there had been less throttle, or if I had assigned myself to Number Two spot. We lost many friends in the War of Attrition; you might say we were well used to suffering. But Shlomo Weintraub was something else. His tragic death was a serious loss to the squadron. He had been a very popular figure. We felt his loss for a long time.

Shlomo's wife was in the advanced stages of pregnancy when she received word of her husband's death. A few days later she went into labour. I took her to the hospital. More than sixteen years have gone by; I haven't forgotten a thing.

Chapter 11
AT TREE-TOP HEIGHT

The late Colonel Ezra 'Babban' Dotan was known in the Israel Air Force as 'Mr Skyhawk'. In all the many hours he logged in the Skyhawk, one story in particular proves how fitting the sobriquet was; it turned Babban, then commander of an A-4 squadron, into the world's only Skyhawk pilot to shoot down MiGs in a dogfight. One of them was downed with air-to-ground rockets, which were never intended for air battles.

After two heart attacks and open-heart surgery, Babban transferred to a transport squadron and continued to fly for the Air Force. He died in 1981. He told the story of the dogfight between the Skyhawk and the MiGs ten years ago.

I was already at the squadron early in the morning, briefing the pilots who were to participate in the flight. We were assigned to provide cover for armour and infantry forces that had crossed into Lebanon, into Fatahland (the popular Israeli name for the area in southern Lebanon then under control of the PLO's Fatah faction). The date was 12 May 1970, at the height of the War of Attrition.

Because it was felt there would be enemy tanks, we were armed accordingly, with rocket pods and cannons. I was leader of the first pair, which was designated to patrol ahead of the ground troops, looking for hostile forces and destroying them.

We flew around over the area, turning in an 'Indian circle' in which one aircraft is always opposite the other, watching

60

out for him and keeping an eye on the ground. We circled like this at a few thousand feet trying to locate tanks. But this was rough terrain, so we descended until we could identify vehicles and determine if they were ours or theirs. While doing this my Number Two saw MiGs down below. Because I couldn't see any tanks or other enemy forces I told him, 'Okay. Put your nose on them and we'll go after them.' Number Two moved out ahead to lead and we began to descend and chase after their planes without my seeing them at all.

I went into the chase with a bad feeling; I had been sent on this mission to cover our ground forces, and my ordnance was specifically for this. I was leaving in the middle to run after a target which might or might not be there. Ground control couldn't tell me anything about MiGs flying around the area, and all my attempts to verify the MiGs' existence were fruitless. On the other hand, my Number Two was enough of a veteran, and I trusted his claim that he had positively identified the MiGs. But the doubts persisted. I asked him again, 'You see MiGs?' At that moment I saw them right in front of me: a pair of Syrian MiG-17s, cutting sharply to the left at low altitude.

By the sharpness of their break I knew I wouldn't be able to get set up on them. I gave permission to fire. Number Two opened up and his shells passed by the tail of one of the MiGs; the tracers told me he had no chance of gaining a hit. In those days the Skyhawks were not equipped with air–air sights; the aircraft were meant for attack, not interception.

I completed my descent towards the MiGs just as they finished their turn. I was now behind them. At this stage in the chase, when I was sitting on their Number Two, I decided to utilize the fire power of the anti-tank rockets. I was carrying five pods, each with nineteen rockets.

I was very close to the MiG, about 130 metres. I hung onto him as well as I could, pressed the firing button, and let loose two pods, thirty-eight rockets, at the same time. The pilot didn't even feel me firing at him; the rockets, which were very heavy, passed underneath and struck the slopes of Mount Hermon. The two MiGs continued on, still unaware that I had fired on them, so I raised my sights a bit and gave him another salvo of two pods. This time the MiG disappeared in a tremendous explosion.

61

At the same second Number Two shouted, 'MiGs behind you!' I broke hard up and to the left and realized I was in a sandwich, trapped in the middle of a formation of MiGs. We had gone for the first two without noticing there were more to the rear. Only at the battle's end was it clear there had been eight.

While breaking I looked in my rearview mirror and saw what was happening. I could see the MiG's tracers going right by above my vertical stabilizer. I was immediately convinced by the way the MiGs were attacking that these were not real professionals. So I calmed down a bit and was already telling myself, 'Here you are; you're going to shoot down your second MiG.'

He passed about fifty metres from me; I could clearly see the Syrian pilot's head. I straightened out to fire at him with my cannons but then saw another MiG at my back. He was about 600 metres away, well set up in ideal firing position. I broke left and down to get away from him. Suddenly I noticed another MiG that had passed by. The pilot went on to afterburner and a large flame shot from his tail. He had apparently decided to run home.

In those days I had my own special Skyhawk. It was the only one with 30mm cannons; the rest had 20mm guns. I decided to knock the MiG down with this airplane and with these cannons.

I was diving towards Mount Hermon, and when I tried to come out of the dive I discovered I was hardly moving. The ground was drawing near but the aircraft would not respond; I would pull back on the stick, but the nose would not come up. I then remembered that the four rocket pods I had fired were now dead weight and a lot of drag. The domed coverings had been blown through and each of the pods had turned into something much like a door. I jettisoned the pods and the aircraft began to climb and gain speed.

I came out of the dive very close to the ground, really at tree-top level. Straightening out to the rear of the MiG I fired a short burst from some 500 metres. This kind of shot had no chance of hitting, but I wanted the MiG to change direction. It was clear that this MiG would not be returning home; it would have to climb over Mount Hermon to get back to Syria and I knew I would be able to cut him off and block his way when he began to climb. I still had a lot of fuel, while the

MiG was getting low because of his afterburner. And I was planning to exploit this to the very end.

My Number Two was flying at a higher altitude, protecting the area to the rear. They were firing at us from the ground with all kinds of weapons, filling the sky with technicolour, but we ignored the turmoil and kept after the MiG, flying north, deep into Fatahland. Meanwhile some of our Mirage pilots had shown up and asked over the radio, 'Where's the fight?' I was afraid they'd go after the MiG, and said sharply, 'Boys, this is my fight. Find yourselves another MiG.'

We were flying very low, so low there was a danger of hitting a tree, a house, or the side of the mountain. In the middle of the chase the MiG began making light turns. Aha, I told myself, the boy in the MiG is nervous and worried about what's going on behind him. Otherwise he'd have no reason to make these moves. I made up my mind that I would now catch him. But just then I lost him in one of the wadis. According to the ground contours we were very close, and a few seconds later I saw him leave the wadi, pulling up quite sharply. If I hadn't known where to look I would have passed him right by with the high speed I had built up during the chase.

I estimate we were flying at a speed of about 520 knots. I immediately did everything I could to slow down and not pass the MiG. I closed down everything I could. I throttled back. I extended my dive brakes. I lowered my flaps. Had it been possible I would have stuck my ears outside the cockpit. I slowed down so close that I couldn't lower my nose enough to hit him. I was also afraid I would be hit myself if the MiG exploded from my fire. I decided to let him open some distance.

The MiG began breaking from side to side until it seemed we were playing cat and mouse. He turned right, with me after him; he turned left and I was right with him. This continued a number of times, back and forth, as the distance between us gradually increased. As soon as I saw I had an acre of MiG in my sights – large enough for it to be impossible to miss – I aimed and fired a long burst, hitting him in his wing root. The wing turned into a sieve; it opened up and tore from the fuselage. The MiG rolled right, hit the ground, and blew up.

We broke left and pulled to altitude, and I asked the

controller if they still needed us to cover the ground forces; I learned that another formation had taken our place at the beginning of the dogfight. We formed up and flew home. Over the base I did a buzz job with two victory rolls. It was a great, joyous occasion; champagne and cake were already waiting for us back at the squadron.

Later I learned that the second pilot I shot down might have been a Syrian squadron commander, a colonel who three weeks before had broken the sound barrier in the skies of Haifa. Why was this merely a possibility? Because there had been another dogfight at about the same time and in the same area where another MiG-17 was shot down by Asher Snir. We learned that the famous colonel had indeed been shot down the same day, so it wasn't clear whether the colonel was shot down by me or by Snir. At any rate my MiG pilot fought very hard under difficult conditions, caught at low altitude, and all this was evidence of his flying ability. The difference between us was that he stuck to his decision to run home, and I stuck to mine to shoot him down. And if you will, that sentence tells the story of the whole aerial struggle between us and them.

Chapter 12
I KNEW YOU'D COME

*Towards the end of the War of Attrition an Israeli Phantom
was hit while on an attack mission on the Egyptian front. The
pilot was taken prisoner while the navigator went into hiding.
An Israeli Sea Stallion helicopter was sent to the area in the
late hours of the night; it located and rescued the navigator
from right in the middle of Egyptian troop concentrations.
The helicopter pilot was Nehemia Dagan, today a brigadier
general, and IDF Senior Education Officer.*

I was put on this war train against my will, and I've been riding
it ever since. The view from the train occasionally changes,
but I ride it reluctantly and have to keep my head up.

Of the stories from the War of Attrition, stories like the
snatching of the Egyptian radar and the blowing up of the
Aswan–Cairo high-tension lines, I think this one is the best
because, after all, what was the radar? All we did was go in,
take it and come home. Same thing with the power lines. But
this story has something human about it.

On 30 June 1970 a Phantom was hit over Egypt. Both
pilot and navigator bailed out of the stricken aircraft near an
area full of Egyptian troops. The pilot, Yitzhak Pier, was
captured by the Egyptians. The fate of the navigator, David
Ya'ir, was still unknown; he had apparently landed a few
kilometres from the enemy troop concentrations. I was told
to go out around midnight, find this navigator, and rescue
him.

I looked over the intelligence map – he was right in the middle of the Egyptian army! To encourage me even further there began a nerve-wracking chain of orders and counter-orders: at 6.30 they told me we were going out with ten soldiers and a medical crew; an hour went by, and with it came a change.

'Listen,' they said, 'we're switching the ten soldiers for ten others.' I understood why and my heart began to sink.

Another hour went by, and another phone call. 'What do you think, instead of ten soldiers we send out just three?'

A few minutes later and again they were on the line. 'Look, we know he's okay, so maybe we'll keep one of the medics behind.'

And me? After every call I got goosebumps.

We took off for the south at midnight in a Sea Stallion specially fitted for rescue duties. We landed at Refidim to take on fuel. I got out of the aircraft and, wouldn't you know it, there was a call for me in Operations.

I lunged for the phone. 'What now?'

'Look,' they said on the other end, 'we want to give Operations the names and serial numbers of everyone flying this rescue with you.'

'Gentlemen,' I replied, on the verge of blowing my top, 'there's a limit even to sadism. If you need to – do it yourselves!'

We took off. The night was pitch black and we had to fly low. We were especially cautious – the ground would be just as dangerous as the missiles waiting in ambush. We crossed the lines and turned south. David Ya'ir had a distress-signal transmitter making harsh beeping noises like the howling of a cat. The helicopter had a direction-finder that pointed towards the area from which the distress signal was coming. Then, when we arrived on the scene, there was a problem.

The direction finder brought you to within 200 or 300 metres of the source of the distress signals. During the day this would be enough for a visual fix, but at night you would need to see some kind of light to zero in on. In fleeing his pursuers David had got rid of every light source he had, and we feared we were going to pass close by and not see him. And indeed, this is what happened.

We made one pass and saw that the direction finder's needle was now pointing to the rear. We turned in our tracks.

But because there was no choice I decided to do something dangerous; we turned on our lights, and in the middle of the Egyptian army was an Israeli Sea Stallion at a height of five or ten metres with two powerful searchlights blazing away and swinging to and fro. We flew around for ten minutes or so and couldn't find him. I had a terrible feeling that he was here and we were going to go home without him.

But now the direction finder was beginning to spin. David could use the distress transmitter as a voice radio as well, and when someone spoke the needle would spin. My spinning direction finder meant he was speaking to me. I couldn't hear him, and for some reason I shouted over the radio, 'He's speaking to me! Can anyone hear him?'

He answered with three words: '90 degrees right.'

I turned 90 degrees to the right and there, in front of the searchlights, stood David, waving his undershirt. When I saw him my hair stood on end – just like it's doing right now.

We landed next to him and swung open the door; he got in and said, 'I knew you'd come for me.'

I told him, 'David, even I wasn't sure.'

'I knew,' he replied, 'that if there was even the slightest chance, you wouldn't leave me here.'

When we entered the area we had alerted the Egyptians to our presence; they saw us searching above them, and when we left they started firing. I've seen a lot of anti-aircraft fire in my life, but I had never seen anything like this. It was like a sea of fire coming up from below. We were flying at a height of 30 feet; I shouted a warning and brought the helicopter up a little, and then back down. We broke left, and we broke right. Finally we said, what are we doing, this will only take more time! So, holding our breath, we flew in a straight line to the east. We passed at low level between the ships stranded in the Bitter Lake since the 1967 war. We crossed our lines. Home. We landed again at Refidim to refuel and checked the aircraft over. Not a single bullet hole!

It was already daylight when we landed back at the base. We opened the door and David got out and fell into the arms of his mother and wife. They walked away from the helicopter, on one side of David his mother, on the other side his wife, who was eight months pregnant. Knowing you brought him out of there – these are the beautiful moments that give you the strength to go on and get the job done.

Chapter 13
UP AGAINST THE MISSILES

During the War of Attrition, Major General Avihu Bin-Nun served as commander of a Phantom squadron. The Phantom squadrons were the Air Force's spearhead at the time and carried the brunt of the fighting in the campaign against the Egyptian missiles. Avihu Bin-Nun's story is wrapped around a certain aspect of the bitter and stubborn struggle between the missile and the airplane – the cost.

This time we went in with everything. For a number of weeks we had been waging a stubborn match: Israeli Phantoms against Egyptian missiles. So far we were the losers. The struggle with the missiles had caused the loss of three aircraft; three pilots and two navigators had been caught by the Egyptians. This had a heavy effect on morale. We went out on this raid knowing that the outcome of the whole struggle would depend on its results. We knew we were liable to pay a steep price; we couldn't imagine how steep it would be.

The first strike had taken place on 30 June 1970. I led a formation of three pairs to Rubeiki, between Suez and Cairo, where there were three SA-2 batteries that the Egyptians had slowly moved up in the direction of the Canal. The missile batteries had started out around Cairo; with time they had been pushed up towards the border. With the batteries' progress northward we soon came to call it the 'Rolling Missile Campaign'.

We crossed the Canal at low level, found the three

batteries, and attacked and destroyed them. There was lots of anti-aircraft fire which we were able to evade. Before recrossing the Canal we were supposed to climb to altitude for about a minute. Rami Harpaz, one of the pilots in the formation, made a mistake: instead of waiting until the Canal he climbed right after the attack. There was another battery we hadn't known about and it launched its missiles at him. His aircraft was hit by two of them, and Rami and his navigator, Eyal Ahikar, parachuted into Egyptian territory.

Yallo was Rami's Number Two. He had seen him climbing at the wrong time and shouted for him to get back down. But it was too late. He saw Rami being hit and bailing out. I was up ahead a bit and saw just the mushroom of smoke from the stricken aircraft. 'Sorry,' Rami told me over his survival radio as he descended beneath his parachute, 'I goofed.'

Another of our Phantoms was hit by missiles that day. The two crewmen, Yitzhak Pier and David Ya'ir, managed to parachute over Egyptian territory. Only after Pier came back did we get the hair-raising story of his fall into captivity. David Ya'ir, the navigator, was safely rescued by one of our helicopters.

From that day on the Egyptians continued to roll their missile array forward, and every day we would attack the batteries of the emplacements that had been prepared for the missiles. All the work was given to the Phantom squadrons. The crews were being whittled down each day, but we gritted our teeth and carried on, paying the price of the struggle against the missiles with our people and our airplanes.

On 5 July I led a two-plane flight on a raid against a missile battery halfway between Cairo and the Canal, near the Cairo-Ismailia road. We went in low and destroyed it. On the way out we were caught by hellish anti-aircraft fire; our exit route was relatively desolate, so we could bail out over it if we were hit. My Number Two didn't head home along this route, taking instead a different direction straight to the Canal. The Phanton flew along with a tail of fire chasing it. One of the missiles struck the aircraft; the plane exploded, and the two crewmen, Amos Zamir and Amos Levitov, parachuted straight into an Egyptian anti-aircraft position and were taken prisoner.

I came back from this sortie to a squadron that was really hurting, a squadron which in a short time had lost two aircraft and four crewmen and had put together a repertoire of gallows humour. There were no longer any protests that this couldn't go on. Against this background was born the attack plan for 18 July.

The Egyptians had already arrived with an array of batteries to within some twenty to thirty miles from the Canal. It was clear our next attack would be a model of power and intensity. It was a bitter mistake not to have done this earlier; we should have exploited some of our lesser successes in which we had destroyed some of the batteries, by coming in at full strength and taking out the whole system. It had been a mistake to settle for isolated strikes against single batteries; in doing so we paid the price but didn't get to enjoy the fruits of our labour.

This time we went in using a new and completely different method: we brought out all the Phantoms we had and planned a massive strike of tremendous intensity, the aircraft being equipped with electronic warfare pods for protection against the SA-2. This time we planned to fly at high altitude, with the wider field of vision this afforded. The EW pods gave us a sense of security, and we had faith in the new tactic.

We staged the strike on Saturday, the targets being five SA-2 missile batteries. Israel's first Phantom squadron leader, Shmuel Hetz, led the initial quartet, which went straight into the missile array. My four attacked immediately afterwards. Three additional formations of four aircraft each waited their turns. As we crossed the Canal we were welcomed by a hail of anti-aircraft fire impossible to describe, at various altitudes and of an unrelenting intensity. There were carpets of shells at altitudes corresponding to their calibres – and SA-3 missiles we hadn't known about. Our warning sets were reporting the various dangers at full tilt, and at a certain point there was no longer any sense in paying attention to them.

I went into the attack with my Number Two, and from a distance I saw missile launches. I noticed an explosion near Hetz's aircraft and saw him pass below me, leaving a trail of smoke; his Number Two anxiously flew around him. We weren't on the same radio frequency so we had no idea what had happened to him.

There were real missiles and decoys, but by the launchings we could determine where the danger spots were. I was highly confident; they fired between forty and sixty missiles at me and I evaded them all. I had enough experience to know exactly what to do in order to identify the missiles and make them miss.

I attacked a battery along with my Number Two and noticed a missile heading out. I warned Two, 'Watch out, missile launching.' We went on to afterburner, accelerated, and waited for visual contact with the missile. The SA-2 is a relatively large missile; I wanted to follow its progress and then break hard so it wouldn't be able to change direction. I did just that, and waited until I could see it at a familiar size. It was already quite close when I realized this was an SA-3, which was smaller and more manoeuvrable. I broke hard, and this saved me from a direct hit. My Number Two, seeing that I had come out of the explosion, went in, bombed and destroyed the battery, and joined back up with me.

About a thousand pieces of shrapnel had hit my aircraft, penetrating the cockpit, the left engine, all the systems and hydraulic lines. I lost all communication with the outside, as well as with my navigator, Shaul Levi. He was an excellent navigator and his presence helped me get through this crazy flight, the likes of which I had never seen.

The first thing I did was get rid of the bombs, which led Shaul to think that another missile had hit us. Using hand movements I signalled him that everything was okay. I forgot to jettison the Sparrow missiles, which were partially recessed into the aircraft's fuselage. The left engine was on fire and making grinding noises; I shut it down immediately. There was also a fire warning light for the right engine, but its gauges were all right. I quickly assessed the situation and decided it would be preferable to return to the squadron back in Israel, and not join the pilots already in Egypt. I hoped somehow to make it past the Canal and then bail out.

Meanwhile, missiles from the other batteries were flying all round us, and I could watch them through the holes in the aircraft. Shrapnel had grazed my clothing, and some of it left scratches on my shoulder. Only one of the three hydraulic systems was working; thanks to it I was able to keep on flying the airplane.

We passed the Canal, and the aircraft was still going. I planned an emergency landing at Refidim. A large part of the left wing was gone, the explosion having been on that

71

side. I wasn't able to fly below a certain speed. I was still very heavy and decided to dump some fuel, but it wouldn't come out because there was no pressure.

When we arrived at Refidim I was able to lower the arresting hook, and got the wheels down with the emergency system. But I couldn't stop. I had hoped that with the drag chute, the emergency brakes and the cable I would make it to a stand-still. I did everything I could, but nothing worked. The parachute tore due to the speed and weight. The arresting hook didn't stop us because there was no cable. I had no brakes. There was a side wind. In short, everything was stacked against me.

We were slowly drifting, with no control over the airplane and nothing we could do. The aircraft simply ran where and how it wanted. We could only pray. Suddenly we left the runway and ran at a crazy speed straight toward Refidim's open area, which was full of potholes and trenches, and piled with the wreckage of burnt-out MiGs. And interspersed between all these obstacles were anti-aircraft positions. The Phantom continued to run through all this in a straight line, and if it hadn't been for the high speed we would already have racked up. We passed every obstacle without hitting a thing. How? I don't know. A matter of luck. And then, as I began to believe in miracles, a soldier who had prepared the emergency net for us suddenly appeared. He apparently didn't understand what was going on; he raised the net, passed within a metre of my wheels, and, luckily, at the last minute, managed to run to the side before the aircraft could roll over him.

The aircraft hit a small rise; the nose was smashed and the front wheel broke. We had stopped. We climbed down from the Phantom, our legs shaking. This was the first contact I had had with Shaul since the Egyptian missile had hit. We looked at each other, then at the airplane, and were stunned: a fire was burning around the Sparrow and the warhead was leaking melted explosives onto the ground. We didn't say a word. We just ran.

We thought we'd be getting a hero's welcome and that we'd be celebrating our miracle all night. But everything was turned upside down in a matter of seconds. We were told Hetz had been killed.

Chapter 14
HETZ HAS FALLEN

The death of Major Shmuel Hetz, the original commander of Israel's first Phantom squadron, left a deep scar. The circumstances surrounding his death remain a mystery to this day. Brigadier General (Res) Menahem Eini was Hetz's best friend and was his navigator on the tragic mission.

It was a tough evening. The phones wouldn't stop ringing and there was an air of nervousness and tension. We were sitting in my house: Rafi Harlev, the base commander, Shmuel Hetz, the squadron leader, and me. We went over the maps for the next day's flight and read the orders once more – there was no doubt this would be the toughest and most complicated mission we'd ever known.

Rafi was vehemently against Hetz and me flying together in the same plane. 'You two possess all the squadron's theoretical and operational knowledge,' he said. 'What will we do if something happens to you?'

He didn't have a chance. We were such good friends that Rafi had no choice but to give in to Hetz's and my stubbornness. In addition, he had taken command of the base barely three weeks before and, as Hetz was so dominant in the squadron, Rafi simply had to pack it in. Hetz won out and the two of us went on the sortie – from which I alone came back, and only after forty months in Egyptian captivity.

Hetz was the most outstanding individual of our age-group in the Air Force, head and shoulders above everyone

73

else. He radiated a special kind of intensity; he was smart and always charming. He was an obvious choice as the first Phantom squadron leader, though it was the first time they had picked someone from the younger generation and not a veteran and more experienced pilot.

We started basic training together, then pilot school. He went on to fighters, I to navigation. After advanced training we split up: Hetz went to Hatzor and I went to Tel Nof. But our friendship was never cut off, and I was quite happy when our paths crossed once more with the arrival of the Phantoms. He was chosen squadron commander and I was appointed senior navigator.

The Phantoms arrived in Israel on 5 September 1969, and a month later we had already gone out on an attack against an SA-2 battery near Port Said. On the way Hetz told me this was his first time crossing the Canal.

During the War of Attrition a tremendous burden had been placed on the Phantom squadrons, reaching its peak three weeks before the 18 July raid. The Egyptians set up a tremendous array of SA-2 and -3 batteries west of Cairo, and had slowly moved them up towards the Canal. Clearly, only Phantoms would be able to take care of these sites, and this concentrated and extraordinary effort against the missiles was dropped in our lap. Again and again we were sent on strikes against areas saturated with missiles, going up against a tremendous mass of threats, being hit and falling, pulverized both physically and emotionally. The tension and exhaustion were keenly felt in the Phantom squadrons. Our flights and attacks against the missiles yielded no results – they simply failed. The blunt reality simply had to leave its mark on the pilots' morale.

Two weeks before the attack there had been an Egyptian missile ambush on some Mirages that were on a recce mission. In reaction, a number of Phantoms were sent to hit the missile batteries that afternoon. Two aircraft were shot down. One of the pilots, Rami Harpaz, was captured. It was against this background that we received our orders for the Saturday 18 July sortie.

The orders, received on Thursday, were simple and concise: the mission would be to strike at surface-to-air missile batteries between Cairo and the Canal, about fifty kilometres west of Suez. A number of Phantom formations were to participate. The designated time for the attack: 12:40.

We went into the briefing at seven in the morning. Hetz, who was to lead, presided. Aside from the tension – which by that time had already become the norm – there was no omen of anything bad. Things went this way dozens of times: target designation, locating and marking them on the maps and aerial photographs, assigning specific objectives, and afterwards, going out to the aircraft, doing the pre-flight checks, and taking off. It was 12:15, it was hot and clear, and dazzling light accompanied our take-off.

The ordnance we were carrying was nothing out of the ordinary, but judging from past experience it was quite efficient: ten 850-pound bombs. Besides the bombs we carried an additional device: for the first time in IAF history our aircraft were equipped with electronic warfare pods which were supposed to offer protection against the Egyptian missiles.

Here I've got to stop a moment to say a few words about this pod. At the time electronic warfare (EW) was in its infancy, not only with us, but around the world. Instructions for the pod's operation came from a US Air Force major. The flight profile he suggested, which had worked for the USAF, bothered us from the outset. We were to fly in pairs at 18,000 feet, in a straight flight path and with a minimum of banking so as not to upset the pod as it interfered with the guidance systems of the missiles being sent up against us. Our pilot instincts rebelled against this flight profile. We felt we would be sitting ducks, flying straight and level at 18,000 feet above the missile nests. But the pod was portrayed as being so efficient – a magic potion against the SA-2 and SA-3 – that we had no choice but to follow the directions and fly accordingly. This turned out to be a fatal error. The EW pod had no capability against the SA-3 missile, and its effectiveness against the SA-2 was very limited. But they told us we had nothing to fear from either missile.

We flew at altitude. Because we were within range of Egyptian radars we didn't even bother maintaining radio silence. We crossed the Canal and flew towards our target, which was about fifty kilometres from Suez.

A few minutes before arriving over target, we received a warning that an SA-3 battery had locked on to us. After a few seconds the battery launched a missile. We saw it closing in but made no attempt to evade it. It was unbelievable how we sat there and didn't lift a finger to save ourselves, believing this stupid pod would do all the work.

The missile, of course, was not impressed by our wonder weapon, coming in underneath us and exploding like they do in the movies.

It felt as if someone had thrown a handful of gravel against the aircraft's skin. There was no sign of fire, no smoke or anything else. Our external communications were the only thing affected; they were completely cut off; we could speak only to each other over the intercom. We immediately released our bombs and banked eastwards towards home. We were already descending and building up speed to avoid any further missile hits. The Phantom, light and descending, reached 600 knots.

We started thinking about friendly fire; we couldn't inform our forces that we were making an unscheduled recrossing of the Canal because the radio was out. We discussed this and decided that, in light of the situation, we'd just have to be careful. We kept talking to each other, perhaps to overcome our anxiety; we exchanged observations, what was happening around us, what we saw, all clear behind us, someone chasing us, no one chasing us. I asked Hetz whether any of his instrument panel warning lights had gone on. He answered that apart from the flight safety warning light – a completely marginal warning apparatus – everything looked normal.

Then, the moment when everything happens at once: just fifteen seconds away from the Canal I noticed the aircraft was slowly rolling left and downward. We were flying at 600 knots and an altitude of just 100 feet. Though I was a navigator, not a pilot, I realized there was no more 'down'. Conclusion: the aircraft was going completely out of control. Without thinking I pulled my ejection handle and flew from the cockpit.

To this day I don't know whether I ejected myself or whether Hetz ejected me a split second before. I'll never know. Even Hetz's death will remain a mystery; we'll never know what happened in that fateful split second. Why didn't he get out? Maybe his canopy was open: with the Phantom, an open canopy prevents ejection. Maybe he was killed getting out. Could be. Hetz took the secret of his death and buried it along with the mashed and smoking Phantom in the sands of Africa. And us, we mull it over to this day without let-up. Why didn't he jump?

When I left the aircraft, we were flying at 600 knots, a tremendous speed, and from the shock of hitting the air I lost consciousness. I remember, as if through a fog, the parachute opening and, afterwards, me crawling wounded on the ground, my left leg with a compound fracture, lying lifeless and askew. My right arm was broken in three places, and I couldn't move this either. There were fractures in other places and I was bleeding heavily from a deep gash in the groin.

The only thing I could do was look around. I saw the mushrooms of smoke given off by our Phantom not far from where I had parachuted. There was no sign of Hetz and I supposed he was dead. I don't know how I did it, but I was able to pull the emergency radio from my overalls and establish contact with a pair of Phantoms in the air. A recording of this conversation, which was quite long, has been preserved. I told one of the pilots that I couldn't see Hetz and that I thought he was dead. I said I was badly wounded, and afterwards reported that I could see a truck-load of soldiers closing in, that they were getting out of the truck, and that they were coming towards me. Of course I couldn't move an inch. I said, 'They're coming closer. Send everyone my best and tell them I'm alive. Goodbye.' I turned the radio off. I think this was the first time anywhere that someone fell into captivity during a live broadcast. As the Egyptians took me away I knew that, back home, they at least knew exactly what had happened to me.

I was released from captivity in November 1973, after the Yom Kippur War. I had sat in an Egyptian prison for forty months, including a year in a military hospital at Ma'adi, and not a day went by without my thinking about the aircraft going down and Hetz's death.

One of the first things I did after being released was to try and determine what happened. Using aerial photographs we located the exact spot where the aircraft fell. This turned out to be within the area on the other side of the Canal that the army occupied during the Yom Kippur War.

We went out there, Rafi Harlev, R (our Number Two on

that raid) and I. We found what we identified as the wheel of a Phantom, strips of cloth from flight overalls and Hetz's remains. We made him a funeral in 1974, and he's buried in Ramat Hasharon, just north of Tel Aviv. The circle had been closed. But the mystery and the wounds remain. Apparently forever.

Chapter 15
A TRAP FOR THE RUSSIANS

In the spring of 1970, Russian intercept pilots arrived in Egypt and took on Egyptian aerial defence duties, save for the area of the Suez Canal. With time, the Soviet pilots extended their flights closer to the front. At first Israel showed restraint, but after repeated Russian attempts to intercept Israeli aircraft, it was decided to set a trap and beat them in a preplanned air battle. Colonel Aviem Sella was then deputy commander of a Phantom squadron and participated in the battle with the Soviet pilots.

For a long time we had been looking forward to doing battle with the Russians and, by a certain point, a fight had simply become a foregone conclusion. The Russians had violated a quiet agreement we had with them, an agreement – unofficial, of course – that they wouldn't penetrate into our territory and we wouldn't penetrate more than thirty kilometres past the front. They violated this fragile agreement twice by trying to intercept our aircraft. The second time came on 25 July 1970, when Russian pilots attempted to shoot down a Skyhawk that was bombing targets in the area of Port Suez. The Skyhawk was hit in the tail, but landed safely within Israeli territory. After this incident it was clear that we couldn't return to the status quo or hold back in the face of Soviet provocations. From that day on a confrontation was only a matter of time.

To my mind, this was the most turbulent period in the

history of the Israel Air Force. We had just started receiving our Phantoms, and in parallel the War of Attrition was building up in intensity. In one year, 1970, we had spread out over a very wide front: recce and other sorties deep into enemy territory; the laying down of sonic booms over Cairo and Damascus; attacks against SAMs, individual and multiple air engagements; development of combat tactics and, for the first time, use of electronic warfare on a massive basis. For us Phantom pilots, it was all new, and was accompanied by growing enthusiasm and appetite. We made impressive strides forward, but also suffered painful failures; one day it would be one big festivity; the next day we'd quietly mourn the loss of a friend. It was a jam-packed and difficult period, at the end of which we would be richer in priceless operational experience.

The decision to go up against the Russians came from the government, and was put in no uncertain terms. Mere contact wouldn't be enough; we were to shoot them down. This was one of the few times that I know of when the government decided in advance to go in at full force, and not just exploit circumstance.

At Operations Branch a plan began taking shape: four Mirages would arrive in the Suez Gulf area, supposedly on a recce sortie. If the Russians fell for it and scrambled, more of our aircraft, Phantoms and Mirages, would appear on the scene to take on the MiGs. The operation was planned for 29 July, but was delayed a day because of hesitation in the political echelon.

The Russian pilot was an enigma to us: we didn't know a thing about him. We did know that the Russians had no battle experience, but we were not familiar with their defensive tactics.

On the afternoon of 30 July, the four Mirages were sent in. They penetrated the Russian patrol zone, some fifteen kilometres from the southern shores of the Suez Gulf and, sure enough, the trap worked. The Russians joyfully scrambled from three nearby bases. The first to arrive were two quartets with the latest model MiGs, and right after them came another two quartets; all shiny with fresh, sparkling paint as if they had just come off the assembly line. They turned in towards the Mirages and dropped their external tanks. The fight was on.

I was mildly surprised because I went out on this mission feeling nothing would come of it. That the operation had been put off for a day, plus the fact that we had been flying a long time, seeing many aircraft on our radar sets but without any engagements, had led me to believe the fight we had been hoping for would not materialize.

I was Number Two in the first pair; the leader was Avihu Bin-Nun. The other pair was led by Ehud Henkin. The distance closed between the Mirages and MiGs. There were dozens of aircraft; the Russians sent in a quartet and then another and yet another quartet, until they reached twenty MiG-21s. Against this we were an even dozen: eight Mirages and four Phantoms. This was the largest air battle yet on the Egyptian front. There were many aircraft in the air, many drop tanks and many missiles. The greatest fear was of getting into a sandwich to collide with another plane.

There was no doubt about one thing: the Russians had been suckered. They figured on dealing with unarmed recce aircraft that they could shoot down at their leisure. Although we were the ones who had set the trap, it was the Russians who initiated the battle. They started it, and by the time they caught on it was too late.

Asher Snir, flying a Mirage, intercepted a MiG, which caught fire within seconds and the pilot jumped from 30,000 feet. This was the scene at the beginning of the fight, and also at the end; the pilot was still dangling in the air some time after everything was over. He floated slowly to the ground, and was the only one to witness the whole encounter. In the heat of battle we used him as a reference point, reporting to one another things like, 'I'm ten kilometres from the parachutist.'

Because of the congestion and multiple targets there were times we actually became a threat to each other. We all fought alone, every man for himself. The Russians manoeuvred alone and in formation, but were never a real threat. They fired plenty of missiles, but without aiming or giving it much thought.

Avihu and I flew around for some time without being able to bear down on one aircraft. Every time we came in on one of the MiGs, another would pull in to our rear. The MiGs fired from every angle and position; it was impossible to catch one without running a certain risk. We got separated very quickly, fearing the battle would end without our shooting down even one aircraft.

I discovered a MiG trying to come in on me. He broke, tried to raise his nose, and made every mistake in the book. He fell for my tricks and came out in front, head-on and high. We began to turn at 15,000 feet. He displayed a very low level of skill. After two or three turns I picked up speed and came down to low altitude. At 2000 feet I reached the desired range and launched a missile, which flew off, arrived on target and caused a great explosion. I felt a lump in my throat. But from out of that great fire came the MiG, in one piece. I fired another missile, but before it struck, the MiG broke apart. The first missile had apparently hit, but I didn't have the patience to wait for results. The pilot jumped. I broke to the side and made sure there were no aircraft behind me.

I turned for home. On the way I saw the fires of other MiGs on the ground. I also saw the parachutist, still floating down, now in the freezing cold of 10,000 feet. I estimate that he was in the air for about half an hour. We had probably already landed, been debriefed and had our coffee while he was still hovering in the air. If anyone wants to know what really happened out there, that would be the guy to ask.

Over El Arish I met up with my leader and saw he was minus two missiles, one Sidewinder and one Sparrow. With my hands I asked him the question: how did you shoot him down? At the time I had a dog called Sparrow, and Avihu answered briefly 'With your dog.'

Of course, there was a great celebration back at the base. We did a victory roll, got drenched on the ground and were given a rousing reception. We were convinced we had downed four MiGs. Later, according to an article by *Al-Ahram* editor Mohammed Hassanein Heikal, it turned out the Russians had lost five aircraft in the battle. It also turned out that the celebration was not ours alone: the Egyptians couldn't contain their glee. Until that air battle the Russians had claimed Egyptian pilots were getting shot down because they didn't know how to use their Soviet-made weapons. After the battle the Egyptians could defend themselves by saying to the Russians: here, even you are getting shot down, and all because of the weapons and airplanes you are giving us!

There was no basis for this claim. The battle with the Russians entailed a trap that worked just like it should, just like in the textbooks. And, above all, this fight pitted our experience against their lack of it. The twelve Israeli pilots who participated had already chalked up fifty-nine aerial victories between them. The confrontation was unavoidable, and it also tipped the scales in the war.

Chapter 16
HIS RIGHT-HAND MAN

On 3 August 1970, during an attack mission towards the end of the War of Attrition, a Phantom flown by Ra'anan Ne'eman and his navigator, Yoram Romem, was hit. Ne'eman lost the use of his left hand and the job of flying was left to Romem. Together they succeeded in bringing the damaged aircraft back from over Egypt to a safe landing. Ne'eman was awarded the Ot Hamofet, *Israel's third highest award for bravery, while Romem was given a commendation.*

Ne'eman From the beginning I had a premonition we wouldn't get out of there. It was really suicidal. It was clear they had set up an ambush and I felt we were going to get hit.
Romem I was a twenty-year-old second lieutenant, the youngest member of the squadron, and maybe the youngest Phantom navigator in the world. Today they wouldn't allow such a youngster anywhere near the briefing room for an operational sortie, but this was my sixth operational flight on the Phantom; there simply was no choice – we had run out of people. For us this was a period of terrible blows; the ranks were thinning out and the squadron was grabbing every able-bodied airman.
Ne'eman We flew out to attack missile batteries near the Canal, north of Abu Suweir. We were Number Two in the formation. The first wave struck and then we went in. Everything had been quiet, but as soon as the leader radioed, 'Going in,' the Egyptian warning system woke up and they

began launching missiles from three batteries.

Romem They launched a salvo of missiles. That was their method; not individual launches, but salvos. The first aircraft, with pilot Yigal Shohat and the Moshe Goldwasser as navigator, took a missile and Shohat immediately called out, 'Number One is hit.'

Ne'eman At that moment I realized we had got ourselves into big trouble. A few seconds later I heard a tremendous explosion. The aircraft lurched and I was thrown against the right side of the cockpit and lost consciousness.

Romem I heard the explosion and saw a blinding light up above. I thought this was a missile that had exploded close by without hitting us. I was certain everything was normal. But suddenly I heard Ra'anan over the radio saying, 'Number Two is hit.' That was how I learned we were in a stricken aircraft.

Ne'eman When I came to I felt heat spreading through my left hand, which had been holding the throttles and was now lying splattered on my belly. Looking at it I was gripped by panic, fear and helplessness. It was crushed and the fingers weren't where they should have been. I became nauseous. I took off my oxygen mask and was overcome by the awful stench of flesh and blood, a stench that was unbearable. I wanted to get out of there.

Romem Sixty pieces of shrapnel had pierced the aircraft. Glass on the gauges in my cockpit had cracked and shattered. I had no idea what was going on in Ra'anan's cockpit. I asked him over the intercom but there was no reply. There was a terrific noise coming over the radio, with everyone yelling at each other. Out of the cacophony of shouts I clearly heard, 'Break! Get out! You're on fire!' I didn't know if this was directed at us or Shohat. I didn't know if Ra'anan was in control of the aircraft. I felt the plane manoeuvring sharply and feared we were going to crash.

Ne'eman During this whole time I had no contact with Yoram. He knew we had been hit and reacted coolly, maybe because he had no idea of the trouble we were in. I looked down to see where I would jump, remembered we were over Egyptian territory and decided I would not be jumping. Whatever happened would happen. I remembered the story of an American pilot in Vietnam who had lost his hand; he was able to keep flying until he reached the sea, and only

85

then did he bail out. I told myself that if he had done that, I could, too.

Romem I heard Ra'anan screaming in pain over my earphones. I still didn't realize he had been wounded. The aircraft was in a steep dive; I told him, 'Watch the altitude,' and I bombarded him with flight data. He thought I didn't understand a thing and was feeding him routine information. The aircraft continued to dive. I thought about my best friend, Amos Levitov, who shortly before had been taken captive. Aha, I said to myself, so this is what it's like when it happens.

Ne'eman Two weeks before I had seen the movie *The Battle of Britain*. The message was: whoever flies in combat for ten seconds without manoeuvring will be shot down. I started going wild with the aircraft. Every five seconds I would pull a manoeuvre. I wanted to speak to Yoram, to tell him to look around and watch for missiles. But I couldn't get even one complete syllable out of my mouth. The best I could do was mutter parts of words.

Romem I heard Shohat over the radio the whole time saying, 'I think I'll make it back to the lines.' But suddenly I saw his plane fall and hit the ground with a great explosion. For a moment there was an overpowering silence on the radio; Ra'anan broke it by saying, 'I think I'm going to bail out.' I assumed the position for ejecting, then asked him if he wanted me to fly the plane. He said no. It was the first time he had spoken to me.

Ne'eman I kept manoeuvring like crazy, the whole time missiles were passing every which way. I couldn't believe the aircraft was holding up and I was constantly telling myself, 'Here it comes. Here it is.' I was in a complete panic. The stink of flesh and blood almost drove me out of my mind. I tried to speak to Yoram but couldn't. I held onto my bad hand with all my strength. It went on and on, and weariness began to take hold.

Romem About a minute before crossing the lines our leader said, 'Maybe you can fly it together.' This helped me become more decisive and I told Ra'anan, 'I've got it.' He agreed. I took the stick and throttles and began to fly. I wasn't worried because the aircraft had finally settled down, and everything seemed fine. Because I was young I trusted in the aircraft; I wasn't aware of any danger. The whole thing was really very exciting; I thought of it in terms of, 'You'll have something to tell the guys.' Through grunts and truncated muttering, Ra'anan explained he was hurt. He was writhing with pain. He had lost three fingers, and shreds of flesh had flown in every direction. He tried to bandage himself with one hand.

Ne'eman After crossing the Canal there were signs of hope. I already didn't care if we bailed out because we were now over our own territory. I took out a bandage, opened it with my teeth, and thought I was John Wayne. I felt a heavy responsibility for Yoram's life; he was very young and inexperienced, and all of a sudden this whole thing had fallen on him.

Romem Back in those days nagivators didn't practise flying. At most we would do it for fun if we were with one of the rowdier pilots. That's why my flying looked the way it did. The first time I changed direction Ra'anan really went nuts, shouting, 'What are you doing? You want to get us killed?' He really scared me. Our objective was to land the aircraft at Refidim. I was in charge of the flying, navigation, and communications. Some of the flight systems had been knocked out, and Ra'anan was afraid the controls would seize up. I wasn't afraid of anything; I had this unbelievable faith in the airplane. I was a kid, simply a kid. This was the first time I was speaking over the radio with ground control, and with excitement in my voice I told the ground that everything was under control and that there should be an ambulance and doctor for Ra'anan. Ra'anan cut me off and said, 'Switch to the tower frequency.' He called himself something I was unfamiliar with; I was sure this was it, that he had gone out of his mind. I told him there was no such frequency. Ra'anan jumped all over me, shouting terribly. I shut up. It was clear the pain had driven him mad.

Ne'eman Suddenly we saw Refidim, and they gave us green flares to tell us we could land. Up to that point I had been planning to show up over Refidim and then bail out. But all of a sudden I felt this great sympathy for the aircraft. I decided to take a chance – I don't know why – and land. I said to Yoram, 'I don't have a left hand. You'll be my left hand.' I took the stick and rudders, and Yoram the throttles.

Romem Because we were under pressure we came in at an angle, a bad approach. Everyone was sure we were going to crash on the runway. I lowered the wheels and flaps with the emergency system. We went around and did a better circuit, with a better approach. They had cleared the runway, and everyone was outside, waiting to see how we were going to crash. We touched down and Ra'anan shouted, 'I've got no brakes!' I yelled back, 'Okay! Pulling the emergency brakes!' I pulled, and the aircraft came to a halt. Ra'anan, because of the pain as well as the excitement, then began to shout, 'Enough! Get me out of here! I can't anymore!'

The crash crews gathered round and didn't know what to do. I tried to open the canopy, but couldn't. I finally forced it open with my arms and helmet and moved up to Ra'anan's cockpit from outside. I opened his canopy and saw what had happened to him. The whole cockpit was red with blood. At the infirmary we hugged each other excitedly. 'You saved me,' he muttered. With a choked voice I answered 'No, you saved me.' The truth was he couldn't have done it without me, and I couldn't have done it without him. Today, understanding more about flying and being under pressure, I realize Ra'anan's behaviour was magnificent.

While still in the hospital Ra'anan decided he would go back to flying. They looked at him a little cockeyed; after all, he had lost three fingers and they didn't believe he could fly with such a handicap. But he did it. He went back to flying and made lieutenant colonel as commander of a Skyhawk squadron. Every once in a while we'd meet and I'd get to know his other side: the lively kibbutznik, laughing and cynical. We didn't get to see much of each other, each of us going our own way. I was surprised to hear one day that he'd found religion. I don't know what he's doing today, but I think that, like me, he'll keep our flight in his heart forever.

Chapter 17
JUMP FOR LIFE

At midday on Friday, 17 September 1971, eight crew members went out in an Israeli Stratocruiser to photograph the Egyptian frontlines in the Suez Canal area. Forty minutes after take off, all that was left of the Stratocruiser were charred and blackened pieces in the desert sands. The aircraft had been caught in an ambush of SA-2 missiles, and crashed 22 kilometres east of the Canal. Only one of the eight crewmen survived; he was the flight mechanic, Major Hanania Gazit.

At 1:47 – for some reason this hour is engraved in my memory – we entered into a turn facing Port Said and going south. We were flying at 28,000 feet in clear and stable weather; the aircraft's performance was smooth; we were shooting the breeze on our plans for the evening. The atmosphere was excellent.

As the clock's hands moved towards H-hour, everyone withdrew into himself, busily preparing for his part in the mission. The aircraft commander made sure everyone was wearing a parachute, that the oxygen systems were hooked up and working properly, and that the intercom was operating. This kept us busy and diverted our thoughts from what might happen. The feeling was that everything was going according to plan.

Suddenly, at 2:10, as we were flying east of the Canal and north of the Great Bitter Lake, there was a thunderous explosion. The Stratocruiser was flung aside with a terrific lurch; there was an immediate loss of control, and we went into a spin. The aircraft became filled with a white mist, and it became difficult to see even my control panel.

My first feeling was one of paralysing fear but, after a few seconds, logic began to take over. Everyone understood that he had to keep at his task, to try and overcome the problem, or to bail out. At first I was stuck to my seat, unable to move; immediately afterwards I found myself hovering at the ceiling, held up by the centrifugal force. I noticed the captain trying without success to get a hold of the aircraft, and heard him shout: 'Out of control! Bail out!'

According to our emergency directives, I had a number of things to do at my control board. Then I began to crawl towards the exit. At the same time I shouted to the others to jump.

The Stratocruiser's emergency exit was on the lower level. To reach it from the crew stations one had to go all the way to the rear of the aircraft, and from there down below, all while the plane was spinning quickly to the ground. On my way to the emergency exit I was thrown around and found myself pinned to the bulkhead. For a long time I was unable to move and thought I had no chance of making it to the emergency exit before the plane crashed. I decided to make for a closer emergency exit, a large window at the wing.

The only thing I thought about while moving towards the exit was how to get out. But, whenever the spin's centrifugal force held me fast and helpless against the bulkhead, I would think about the worst thing of all, my wife and my daughters, and the sorrow I would be causing them, and how terrible this all was.

During my efforts to reach the exit I met up with only one other crew member, and only for a few seconds; it was clear he had listened to me and was going to join me.

I looked for the over-wing exit, and after a great effort I reached it. I was able to pull the handle, and the air pressure sent the panel inwards. Above it I saw the wing and two engines.

The strong air currents swirling around outside made it difficult for me to get my body through the opening. After a great effort I was a third of the way out. Then the air currents pulled the rest of me; I had been sucked out, and found myself in mid-air. Miraculously I was not struck by the spinning plane.

Immediately I lost sight of the aircraft. It became easier to breathe; after the Stratocruiser lost cabin pressure the lack of oxygen had blurred my senses. The air spun me around, and I couldn't judge my altitude. At any rate I seemed to be pretty high up; I decided not to use my parachute's barometric control, which would have opened it at 10,000 feet, and pulled my ripcord manually. The chute opened right away. I looked down and saw black smoke rising from the ground; glancing around, I searched for other parachutes in the air. I was drifting towards the flames, but by pulling on my shroud lines I was able to avoid landing in the fire. I came to earth just a few metres from where the plane had hit, and had no idea whether this was in our territory or that of the enemy.

I tried to get close to the inferno to look for survivors. The flames were spread out over a wide area, and every once in a while there were small explosions. My efforts were futile. Parts of the aircraft were scattered over hundreds of metres; nothing was left whole.

After a few minutes I heard a helicopter and looked for a hiding place, fearing this might be the enemy. Luckily it was one of ours. Only when I was aboard the helicopter did I notice that I had been hurt in a number of places. I asked the pilot to go over the area for other survivors; we turned up nothing.

When I got home in the evening I didn't know how to tell my wife what had happened. The bandages were underneath my clothes. At first glance it was impossible to notice a thing. I sent my daughters to a neighbour's and told my wife. She broke into tears. Afterwards I told the girls. They couldn't understand.

The only things left are the memories; a blackened piece of wreckage; a large album whose black pages contain yellowing newspaper clippings with pictures of the seven crew members who perished, arranged according to how they sat before the explosion, and with their death notices alongside; papers from the investigations; a tiny label from my parachute, with the routine signature of the girl soldier who packed it.

The seven crewmen killed were Major Efraim Magen, Major Ze'ev Ofer, Captain Amos Guy, Captain Yoram Heidt, Captain Eliav Inbal, Sergeant Major Yitzhak Tamir, and Corporal David Seri. May their memory be blessed.

Chapter 18
SEVEN MUSHROOMS OF SMOKE

At the Air Force's Sharm e-Sheikh base, the Yom Kippur War begin with a massive attack by seven quartets of Egyptian MiGs. Against this, two Israeli Phantoms were able to scramble. Captain N was pilot of the first Phantom. For his part in the battle for Sharm he was awarded the Ot Hamofet.

On the last night before the Yom Kippur War we sat in the ready room talking quietly. I had done someone a favour by agreeing to go down to Sharm in his place. Along with me came S, at the time a young Phantom pilot, who had also replaced some other flier. We were both there by chance and couldn't have imagined that the long arm of fate would have such a drama in store for us the next day.

The alert was completely routine; no one saw any special importance in it. The last thing on our minds was war, and somehow we were feeling a little distant and lonely. The chances of our coming under attack were unthinkable.

We woke up on Saturday morning at 10.00, and were told that Colonel Yak Nevo would be taking command of the base. We were greatly surprised. Yak landed at one in the afternoon. His second sentence was: 'It looks like the Egyptians are going to start a war.' Before he could finish, the sirens rent the air. This was the opening of the Yom Kippur War.

We were the pair on alert; I was Number One and S was Number Two. We ran to the aircraft. The controller

Brig. Gen. Herzel Budinger, 1986

Maj. Gen. Avihu Bin Nun
IAF Commander

Maj. Gen. Ran Goren
– IDF Chief of Personnel

Mirage circa 1967

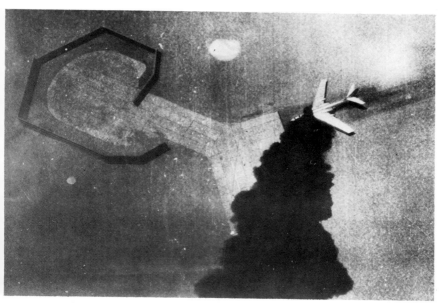

Tupolev bomber burning on Egyptian air strip, 5 June 1967

Phantom with bombs

Phantoms over Jerusalem

F4 Phantom

F4 Phantom

Receipt of first Phantom, 1969, by Golda Meir
and Moti Hod – then air force commander

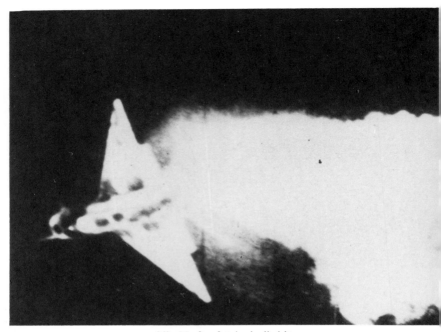

Mig 21 after fatal missile hit

F 16

F 15

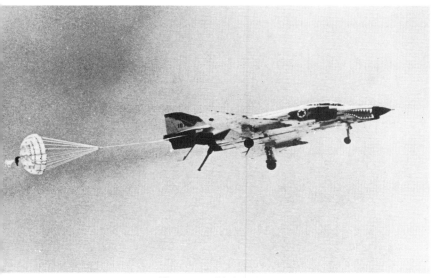

Phantom with bombs

Phantom with bombs

Phantoms in a southern base near Sinai

informed us of dozens of targets over the sea, and I told Number Two: 'That's it, I'm taking off.' I decided to take full responsibility and not wait for instructions. I was still running up the engines and the aircraft was leaving the runway when I looked back to see whether Number Two was taking off with me – and my eyes popped out: smoke was mushrooming from the runway and the sound of a great explosion shattered the air. I remember shouting, 'They are bombing the runway! It's really war!' The aircraft gathered speed but I couldn't take my eyes off the runway below. The Egyptian bombs had dug craters and holes; it's a shock to take off when the runway is being bombed; it's like burning all your bridges behind you – and it's not in some fable.

From that point on I remember only individual pictures. I climbed hard to the rear while letting go of my drop tanks. I descended for a short pass on a MiG-17, which was coming out of a bombing run on the runway. It went low and tried to get away; I launched a missile and the MiG exploded.

The sky was full of airplanes. Three MiGs tried to get on my tail and fired bursts from their cannons. I broke hard and the shells went by. One MiG fled. I went after the other two and they descended to about fifty metres, maybe lower; the chase took us below the base's antennas and power lines. One MiG broke hard, lost altitude, ran towards the sea, and disappeared into the water. This left one more in my sights.

This MiG pilot was the stiff-necked type: he pulled some serious Gs – with me right behind. Once one of the Phantom's engines flamed out; I quickly began losing height. I was almost on the deck when the engine suddenly came back to life. Right away I climbed: there was no time to rejoice in having gotten out of that. I was now working automatically, without much thought.

I remember sweating inside that cockpit and trying to convince myself that I simply had to get out of this fight alive. I really wanted to win.

One of the MiGs came in on me from above and tried to set himself up on my tail. I told my navigator, 'Don't look back.' I got myself on his tail with a great loop and fired a cannon burst. I saw the shells running towards him – and he didn't blow up. I decided to gamble my last missile; the MiG was hit and crashed on the beach.

Suddenly the area was totally quiet. I noticed seven

mushrooms of smoke spiralling above the gulf, testimony to the past few minutes. Number Two informed me there were no aircraft left in the air. We were out of fuel and ammunition, and went in to land.

Finally I saw the craters on the runway, and we landed carefully so as not to fall in. The control tower was empty, its window blown out, and a huge unexploded bomb lay on the runway facing the intercept stand. The sirens wailed without end. The base was already full of people running around; we were welcomed with hugs of joyous shock.

When we got out of the aircraft the base commander, Yak, went over to Number Two and simply asked, 'How many?' Number Two answered, 'Seven: me, three, and Number One, four.' Yak didn't believe him. He simply couldn't believe it.

Chapter 19
TO THE HORROR,
TO THE OUTCRY

The eighth of October, 1973 was considered the most difficult day of the Yom Kippur War, at least for the Israel Air Force. As opposed to its combat doctrine, the Air Force had to go up against Syrian missile batteries without any preparation, and before achieving air superiority. Brigadier General (Res) Yiftah Spector tells the story.

The change came suddenly.

In the morning we were still attacking Beni Suef and Bir Araiyida air bases in Egypt; other aircraft were softening up the Canal line. We were right in the middle of preparing to carry the war to the Egyptians. Suddenly there was an important notice: a change in missions. Everyone, with utmost urgency, was going up against Syria to strike at the missile batteries arrayed around the Golan Heights. The urgency was so great that the strike would be carried out with no preparation or softening up; we went straight to outfitting the attack craft for bombing the missile sites.

There was no time for preparation. In fact, we didn't need any: pre-determined battle plans were snatched from desk drawers; sealed envelopes were ripped open; maps were passed out; a few words were hastily spoken. We ran to the aircraft, getting our final instructions on the way.

Attacking a missile array is no joke. It's a complicated operation based on precise co-ordination and great numbers of airplanes, each covering the other right down to the

95

second. The formulation and drawing up of the plans had been the labour of years – but had never before been tried. Now everything was going out of the window on the galloping legs of dozens, maybe hundreds of pilots who were running to their aircraft on a wild scramble whose single import was for these men to get to where they were going as quickly as possible. The feeling in the air was that there was a fire to be put out.

Aircraft begin scrambling from their revetments, taxiing out and joining into formations at the end of the runway. In the front cockpits the pilots feverishly go over the aerial target photographs they had been given just a few minutes before. In the rear cockpits the navigators memorize their flight routes and mark features that will help them identify the area.

Pair by pair the planes straighten out and take off, heading north at very low altitude. My turn is coming – but wait, they're holding me up. A minute before I'm to mount the runway someone shows up in a jeep, speeding like crazy; he jumps out and waves his arms. I open the canopy; he comes up and gives me new maps and aerial photos and tells me my objective has been changed. Right away the two aircraft that have been assigned to me arrive; we straighten out, open our throttles and take off.

In the air, an armada of airplanes streams northward; there is a trail of black smoke from the Phantoms all along the Jordan rift. Aircraft join up and overtake one another along the way, everyone trying desperately to regulate his speed so that he'll adhere to the time alloted to arrive over the target. Because everybody took off helter-skelter, some are flying at breakneck speed and passing their buddies, while others fly as slowly as possible, as if trying to stand still in the air.

We quickly catch up with and overtake a formation of tiny Skyhawks vigourously paddling northward with all their might. In front of us, behind us and to the sides, singly, in pairs, and by threes, aircraft weave in and out, join up, break away, the course for all of them – northward, northward. And everything is done in absolute silence – not a single word comes over the radio. A great stream of aircraft flows in complete silence, northward.

In the rear cockpit, Arel puts all his effort into learning the map, which he first saw in the moment before I opened up the throttles for take-off. In the front cockpit, I try to keep looking around to avoid a collision in the bustling avenue of aircraft, and turn the aerial photograph of the target over and over, having a hard time lining it up with the north, with the map, with the drawing; I try to digest the landmarks and to transform them into tangible and understandable objects.

We haven't even caught our breath and we're already at the point where we're supposed to turn; we leave the stream flowing north and head out our own way – eastward. The navigator leads us on a flanking approach, beyond the missile array and from the rear.

We cross into Jordanian territory and scrape along the ground. The two other members of my formation follow, pulled back far to the rear. Elad is to my right, Gilutz to my left. We're all flying as low as we can, and our eyes are searching all around.

A deep ravine goes by, and we're over Syria. It's easy to differentiate between Syrian territory and the Jordanian heights. Here in Syria the colours are dark. The ground is strewn with basalt rocks; the earth is black and blossoming with fields of briar; villages of clay, of straw and black rock, low and tiny, are scattered all around. Roads, which are narrow, winding, and almost hidden, are coloured like the rest of the area. From our low altitude we can see only the most limited view, which flows and changes beneath us at tremendous speed.

Almost right away we're lost. Everything looks the same and there's no difference from village to village, from road to road, from one briar patch to another. There are no outstanding features; the ground is a monotony of cracked earth, boulders and briars. We go on with our dead reckoning, trying to be as precise as possible in heading and speed – and this is quite difficult during such a low and tense flight. We rely on our watches and on the precision of my flying, and look for our turn-off – an intersection that should be coming up in just a few more seconds.

In the back, Arel is struggling desperately with the navigation, and gives his all in identifying something safe and sure. Once, he thinks he has picked out some nothing of a ground feature, only to discover right away that it's an error and that, in essence, there is no way to find anything that stands out.

Two minutes out and we make our final preparations. Switches are checked, the orange lights are on, everything's okay. We're still heading north east and it's time to turn. With an even and measured bank we head left, our low wing virtually scraping the dry ground.

The engines are up to full power and the aircraft pushes and accelerates to full speed. We straighten out and race to the north west. Our heads strain forward and we break on to the Heights, which are strewn with troops. A road passes by underneath, a small village to the right, another village farther away. A small army camp. Vehicles. Electric pylons. An intersection.

Arel breaks into a joyous shout; he thinks this is the place he has been trying so hard to hit; our dead reckoning has been precise and has brought us close enough. As for me, I no longer keep an eye on the map; instead, my eyes are stuck on the vista before me, looking for the hair-trigger threat ready to break loose somewhere ahead. Arel quietly steers me with short directives, and I follow them. A top-flight and veteran navigator, he is totally absorbed in bringing us in on the most precise route. His professional reputation is on the line, and right now he's more concerned with this than with the dangers that lie ahead.

Another minute to target – and the silence is suddenly shattered: the radio is filled with shrieks. The eye immediately notices the first missiles, far north to our right, being sent skyward and exploding shortly thereafter in starry flashes. The area around us is still quiet; our time has not yet come and we streak forward deeper into the hostile territory.

The shrieks over the radio increase, and the noise in the earphones is horrible. The voices are high-pitched, tense and heartrending. A flood of instructions all jumbled up: different voices calling to one another, warning, directing, questioning, shouting; all together they produce an awful, hysterical and indecipherable cacophony.

Here and there are pillars of smoke; the first bombs are already shattering the area. Missiles are now everywhere; we can't see any aircraft, just the trails of the missiles, which cross and explode like fire in the heavens. Suddenly there's an awful blaze in the air; a cloud of fire and black smoke billows high up in an awful ball.

Our target is already apparently close, but neither of us is sure exactly where we are. For a moment we hesitate, not knowing what to do. I carefully start to climb and feverishly scour the whole area around me, hoping to find something, ready to defend myself against whatever there is. My mouth is dry and my ears are ringing; the awful shrieks still reverberate within.

Suddenly there's a flash close by on the left; a missile is launched from the ground and passes in front, speeding north in a long flame. Right behind is another, a third and a fourth. The source is immediately evident, standing out on the ground. With the insane speed at which we're rushing forward I can't make out any details; just a round, orange splotch with a number of black spots which look like vehicles. My eyes are drawn to the flames of the missiles, and suddenly I notice a lone Phantom at full bank, high and far to the north, its white belly shining against a background of grey sky. At this moment the missiles arrive, one after the other and he's lost between the explosions – before I even have a chance to warn him, to scream, to shout.

Stick full in the stomach! I pull high and roll over. Now I can make out my target, the missile batteries. With one glance I see the levelled site, a few vehicles in the middle, narrow paths leading to small surfaces with other vehicles. A full missile battery suddenly stands out, a single organic unit, clear and prominent – not another amalgamation of scattered parts. Here it is, and we're right above it. I jerk the plane over on its back, pull in, and we're diving. I aim for the centre. Arel locks in the radar and with a quiet voice calls out the altitude. A moment before the reticle comes on cue, more missiles are launched; they pass on their way somewhere under the Phantom's belly.

And here I press the bomb release.

A short whistle and the whack of bombs falling away, heavy and clear. The aircraft is now light and skittish; it picks up tremendous speed towards the ground; with all my strength I pull back and come out, pass over the target and dip my left wing at full bank. To the rear the two of us see the string of bombs breaking into a cloud of heavy grey smoke. A missile or two still rise and climb skyward like tongues of flame, spinning in their flight; they pass far from the plane behind me, which is pulling out of its dive. I can already see the third aircraft dropping its load on the missile battery –

99

and we're already too far away to see the impact.

South! South! The drama melts away beyond the low and blackened hills, and only a heavy cloud of smoke marks the site of the short battle. There's nothing to do but race southward, zigzagging vigorously between the sparks of the anti-aircraft guns, which have now come to life. And all the while the radio shouts and wails, screams and shrieks, until it runs out of breath.

Chapter 20
COMMANDO ATTACK

On the first day of the Yom Kippur War an Egyptian commando attack was repulsed in the Sinai, and the pilot and navigator of an Israeli Phantom won a commendation for their part in the fight. One of the Egyptian attack helicopters a Mi-8, was left behind and was eventually restored to flying condition in the Israel Air Force. In the first part of this chapter the Phantom pilot, Colonel A, tells of the battle against the Egyptian commando. In the second part Colonel (Res) Eliezer 'Cheetah' Cohen tells about the 'maiden flight' of the Egyptian-Israeli helicopter.

The arithmetic was simple: twelve helicopters, each carrying twenty-five soldiers made a force of 300 commandos. The thought that such a force could have made it to the tranquility of Refidim gives me goosebumps to this day.

This was a real commando attack. Dozens of Mi-8 helicopters took off from across the Canal minutes before dusk on the first day of the war, 6 October 1973. They planned to land hundreds of troops at key points in Sinai: the Mitla Pass, Ras Sudar and along the Refidim–Tasa road. It would be difficult to predict what the war's outcome would have been had the Egyptians succeeded.

We came on the scene at the eleventh hour; some of the helicopters were already on the ground and commandos were disembarking. It was a matter of minutes. If we had shown up a little later, the commandos would have been far away and covered by distance and darkness.

We had been on patrol over Refidim area. M, the navigator and I were in one aircraft and D and Y were in the other. I had three drop tanks while D had just two – a fact that would soon become critical. In the meantime we were just flying around and looking down on the results of the first air attack against Refidim. As for other aircraft in the skies, there were none.

By now D was already aware of the situation on his fuel gauge. It was a little before six in the evening, approaching last light. Suddenly a sign of life from the controller. Something was happening around Ras Sudar; his radar scopes were full of 'little specks, apparently helicopters'. D was in a dilemma: if he remained at low speed to save fuel he'd miss the confrontation. If he hurried, he'd run out of fuel.

We were flying low and made both radar and visual contact with a large number of helicopters crossing the Canal toward Ras Sudar from the south. We let the first ones go – they had already managed to make it some distance – and advanced towards these closer to our emplacements; we struck exactly above Ras Sudar.

Till now, we had no experience in attacking helicopters. The type of attack, of course, influences the choice of sights, the kind of ordnance, and the way of carrying it out. Our lack of experience made it difficult to maintain visual contact with the helicopters and as a result, our first passes were imprecise. We related to the choppers as aerial targets and tried to hit them with missiles. I seemed to get no hits; only later did I learn that I was mistaken. At any rate we decided to save our missiles and try to down the helicopters with gunfire. There were a lot of them; they took evasive action and it was difficult to tell when we were hitting and when we weren't. As the battle developed, we began getting victories.

We tried to exploit what little fuel we had left. It was clear that every helicopter set alight would cause others to panic and run. Over the radio I asked for help from anyone in the air. Two Neshers – Israeli-made upgraded Mirage 5s – succeeded, despite poor visibility, to shoot down a helicopter. You must understand that a contest between a fighter and a helicopter is not at all equal. Strangely enough, the helicopter's slowness is its best weapon.

A number of the Mi-8 pilots pulled fine evasive

102

manoeuvres close to the ground, turning their landings to apparent advantage. One of them manoeuvred so beautifully that in no way could I bring him down with cannons. In the end I passed over him at low speed and then went into afterburner. The blast caused him to lose control and I saw the helicopter crash into the ground.

All together on that day I shot down five helicopters.

One of the Mi-8s not shot down by the Israelis made a hard landing below Santa Katerina Monastery. The pilot got his front wheel caught in a small ravine and broke it. When the gear collapsed, the nose hit the ground and the windshield shattered. The pilot got out to check the damage; the nose-down attitude changed the angle of the main rotors and they struck and killed the Egyptian. The rotor continued turning for a few more hours, until the fuel ran out and the engine stopped running.

When Israeli forces arrived on the scene, the helicopter appeared to be airworthy and it was decided to try and fly it to an Israeli air base. The mission was assigned to Colonel Eliezer 'Cheetah' Cohen.

After a preliminary stroll around the helicopter and a brief inspection, I returned to Air Force staff and began collecting technical material on the Mi-8. The theory didn't take long, nor did I have any particular difficulty understanding the basics of operating this helicopter. At the same time a technical crew went to work on the aircraft, draining the lubricants, running up the systems, and checking the rotor.

I made two run-throughs on the ground: I started up, shut down and started up again. The rotor and main steering mechanism, pedals, stick and controls all worked as they should. The only problem was the emergency procedures and I decided to take along a captured Egyptian pilot. The pilot was highly suspicious of this adventure and asked about fifty times what we were planning on doing with the smashed helicopter. We finished the review by evening and all the crewmen travelled to Refidim to get a few hours' rest.

The next morning we went back to the helicopter. I sat down inside, with the captured pilot, and began setting up the pre-flight check. The mechanics had attached a tyre horizontally to the nose so I'd have something to land on in place of the broken front wheel. The windshield was smashed and I knew I'd find myself in a cloud of dust right at the beginning of my take-off. To keep the dust to a minimum I immediately went vertical (I still got a face full of sand). At 200 feet the cloud thinned out; I went over to horizontal flight towards Refidim – and was amazed. This helicopter had tremendous power! No matter how much I throttled back, this thing went like mad. G, the pilot of the Bell escorting me for the duration of the flight, yelled over the radio that I was flying too fast.

I climbed to 8000 feet so I'd be able to make a forced landing if I had an emergency. Suddenly, Israeli ground troops started in with anti-aircraft fire; they were sure the Israeli Bell was chasing after our Mi-8, which of course was in Egyptian colours.

The Bell pilot made contact with the ground forces and informed them of our position: the ack-ack ceased. From here on in the flight was uneventful although the Egyptian pilot would not calm down; he muttered to himself without let up. I think he was somewhere between praying for a safe landing and raining blessings on the State of Israel.

Although it sounds simple, flying a Soviet helicopter is not at all easy for someone used to flying Western equipment. The Mi-8 presents a mirror image of Western helicopters: the rotor turns the opposite way; the throttle twists in the reverse direction, so that you throttle back when you want to open up. The steering is difficult, the gears are hard, the gyro is huge. But when I overcame all the teething problems, I even began to enjoy the flight.

We were soon approaching the base where we were supposed to land, and the Egyptian suddenly grabbed the controls. 'What's wrong, my friend?' I asked and he answered, 'Landing a Mi-8 is the most difficult part. You can't do it.' I told him I had already been flying for an hour and that I had a lot of experience in helicopters. But he wouldn't back down. In the end I decided to let him land the helicopter. Why not? I had flown with students worse than him.

And then, while descending towards Refidim, the Egyptian panicked and began shouting 'We're going to crash!' I tried calming him down, but without success. He hovered high. I told him where to go, but he headed in another direction.

Somewhat forcefully I took the controls, came in on a shallow approach, did a short hover and settled on the tyre they had attached below the nose. The Egyptian unbuckled his seatbelts and shot outside like a missile.

We refuelled without leaving the cockpit. We were still taking on fuel when Benny Yosefon, a known helicopter freak, ran up to me and begged me to take him along for the rest of the flight. I was a little reluctant, but let him come and we took off from Refidim for home. During this part of the flight I really fell in love with the helicopter. It was powerful, simply massive and once you were well acclimatized it was very easy to fly. A real workhorse. Near El-Arish, when I was feeling confident, I went over to very low level flight, really on-the-deck and Benny and I enjoyed ourselves like a couple of kids. Because of the difference in speed, I had to circle back every once in a while and round up G in his Bell.

I got to the base tarmac in a low hover and saw that, for my landing, they had prepared a wheel that was three times too big. Benny jumped out and hauled over a smaller wheel. I settled on to it and switched off the engine. Now I had only one problem: how to survive all the mechanics who had fallen all over me and were literally smothering me with hugs and kisses.

In the end, new tyres were specially made and parts were collected from the remains of other Mi-8s so the helicopter could be maintained. In this way the aircraft remained flyable and it made dozens of flights in the colours of the Israel Air Force.

Chapter 21
BOMBING SYRIAN GHQ

On the fourth day of the Yom Kippur War a formation of Phantoms was sent on a sensitive and daring mission: to bomb the Syrian military headquarters in the heart of Damascus. At the end of the war, Lieutenant Colonel L, leader of the mission, was decorated with Israel's highest award for valour, for a perfect attack despite the poor weather and heavy anti-aircraft fire.

In the early morning of 9 October 1973 all the pilots and navigators going on the mission gathered in the briefing room. We went over the maps and marked everything we needed. I personally had assigned the crews to the aircraft and knew their abilities. Aware of the responsibility placed on their shoulders, I knew that fear and the instinct for preservation fade before one's willingness to endanger himself and carry out the mission. But one thought kept racing through my mind: flying like this, loaded with bombs, to the heart of Syria – to Damascus – was madness.

We understood the mission's importance from the outset. Rarely does a pilot know ahead of time the specific weight of his own mission within the general framework; he usually goes out to attack his objective without knowing how the raid fits into the overall picture. There are isolated instances in which a pilot goes out on an especially important sortie, when it's clear that success or failure will affect the whole battle: the bombing of the Syrian GHQ in Damascus was one of these.

The situation on the northern front wasn't encouraging, to say the least. The first two days of battle were among the toughest the IDF had ever known. Opposite the great Syrian war machine stood a much smaller Israeli force, which after two straight days of beatings and attrition was showing signs of weakness. The Air Force had been involved in a mutual blood-letting with Syrian armour which had broken into the Golan Heights. We knew that a successful strike against the Syrian nerve centre, the General Staff, would interrupt its command capabilities, affect co-ordination among its field units and increase the confusion. And no less important, it would serve as a clear warning for the Jordanians to stay out of it.

But how do you do it? Syrian GHQ was located in the heart of Damascus, amid thick anti-aircraft defences including ground-to-air missiles; adding to our difficulties, the weather conditions were especially hostile – clouds, storms and strong winds.

Near the end of the briefing, the base commander gave a short talk of his own. I remember his words as if I heard them just yesterday: 'Remember that the mission's success means breaking the nerve centre of the Syrian command. Failure could just throw more fat on the fire.' After this a number of senior army officers added their message – that this mission was of utmost importance.

We go out to the aircraft. I check my Phantom over with more diligence than usual. Over and over I ask myself whether I've forgotten anything. I'm a little worried about the missile belt surrounding Damascus; the other anti-aircraft weapons don't worry me at all, but I've become acquainted with missiles in the last two days. Then there's the fear of the unexpected, of the hidden problems the mission will pose. I know that any navigational error, even of just one kilometre, will be fatal. It's clear that as mission leader I am carrying the heaviest burden.

We climb into the aircraft and take off; now I have to concentrate on the mission itself. I'm a machine: hand on stick, eyes on dials, concentrating on the here-and-now; it would be very easy to lose my powers of concentration if I let my thoughts wander even a little. Have to get over the fear, suppress my thoughts and summon all my knowledge and experience to carry out the mission smoothly.

We cross the lines. The weather gets worse from moment to moment; the clouds pose unacceptable flying conditions and greatly increase the chances for our being discovered by the Syrians. And now we hit an area totally socked in and it's impossible to navigate any farther. We're facing a crisis; under these conditions I have serious doubts as to whether we'll make it to the target. There's a feeling that everything's gone down the tubes and that we're just knocking our heads against the wall.

My immediate instincts tell me to turn around and go back – not needlessly endanger the formation. But if we return now who will carry out the strike? The target is too important to surrender to the dictates of weather. I weigh the choices and decide to take a chance, calling over the radio that we're going on to the target, no matter what.

We come out of the clouds at a place we hadn't planned on: we've strayed from our flight path. Luckily I'd prepared an alternative reference point in case of navigational problems and, indeed, I identify it. With this we head on to Damascus. From above the Syrian capital looks like a large city-village. I don't trust the quietness and it's difficult to explain why.

We had planned a surprise attack – and surprise it is. We pass over an ack-ack position which swings its barrels but can't get in a shot. A shoulder-launched Strella missile passes close by my aircraft and continues on its way. That's it; now we're right over the objective. I go in first, with the rest of the formation behind and the surprise is complete. There are no sirens before the first bomb hits the heart of the camp. One after the other the Phantoms drop their bombs. The hits are precise; a small, but unmistakeable cloud of smoke rises from the GHQ compound. (After the war we learnt that we had hit the roof of the Syrian General Staff building and caused serious damage. Air Force HQ next door was hit only in the upper floors. Five Israeli PoWs were in the basement. When they returned home they told how their Syrian interrogators were convinced that the partial damage to their HQ had been on purpose so as not to harm the Israelis.)

Now our mission is to get away as quickly as possible. The surprise is gone – and a tremendous number of ack-ack guns begin spitting fire. The shooting is wild, without aiming, but sheer intensity takes its toll: one of our aircraft takes a direct hit and falls in Syrian territory. The pilot, Dov Sapir, is killed, while the navigator, Ya'acov Ya'acobi, is taken captive. A second aircraft is hit in the wing and an engine.

We speed home with the damaged airplane. With heavy hearts we maintain radio contact. I fly alongside at a few hundred metres, but there is no way I can help aside from sending a few comforting words over the radio. I remember the stories about being taken captive and about Syrian prisons. Flying over Syria, sitting quietly in the cockpit, you can't help doing this.

In the end we make it home – including the damaged aircraft.

After the war I was told I was going to get a medal. I asked, 'Why me? Why not someone else? The flight belonged to all of us, pilots and navigators alike.' I went up to receive the commendation with tears in my eyes; a number of faces were missing from the large audience of military personnel, civilians and families – those who didn't make it through the war.

Chapter 22
GUNS ON JEBEL ATAQA

In the first week of the Yom Kippur War, Lieutenant Colonel Y, then commander of a Sea Stallion helicopter squadron, carried a small force on an unusual mission to the western side of the Suez Gulf, behind enemy lines. Bringing the force back safely turned out to be the most difficult part of the operation.

It was the first week of the war, the Egyptians had already crossed the Suez Canal along its entire length and had established bridgeheads on our side. I commanded a squadron of Sea Stallions. My mission was to fly, in two Sea Stallions, two 105mm M109 cannons and land them – with crews on the summit of Jebel (Mount) Ataqa, west of the Suez. The mountain was not yet in our hands; it was still in the heart of Egyptian concentrations, deep behind the lines. The cannons were to shell the Suez-Cairo road and then be brought back the same way they went in, by Sea Stallions.

The unknown outweighed the known – and we lacked one particularly important piece of data; the on-site temperature. As the temperature rises, a helicopter's carrying capability drops; not knowing the temperature at the landing site made it difficult to decide on the weight of the equipment we would take. After we arrived at Refidim, with our load, it turned out that it would be very hot. We had to leave behind some of the ordnance.

At nine-thirty in the evening we took off with the cannons, their equipment and crews. Turning south towards

Ras Sudar, we made contact with our own anti-aircraft units and, after a great effort, informed them of our passing through and continued on our flight. Over Ras Sudar we turned west, crossed the Red Sea and flew north along the coast at low altitude. Coming in on Jebel Ataqa from the south, we could make out a large Egyptian army camp spread out on the slopes of the mountain.

At the site it turned out the area was too rocky and not suitable for landing. The gunners also realized that it would be impossible to drive in the stabilizing stakes of their guns. This possibility had been anticipated. The artillery commander happened to be a geologist; from study of aerial photos before take-off he had predicted rocks and prepared an alternate site. We now headed in that direction, landed and unloaded the guns.

According to plan, the guns were to fire for fifty minutes and then pack up. The firing began as planned and we circled above the southern slopes, watching from a distance and waiting for word from the artillery men to go back and pick them up. At first everything went exactly as planned. The cannons fired and the pick-up call came on time. Good, the business was finished and we were going home. But in reality, things hadn't yet begun.

Apparently because of humidity, a thick black cloud hung right over the area after the bombardment. The cloud covered the summit and I suddenly found myself inside it. I made it out and hovered nearby, waiting for the cloud to disperse, then climbed and turned a bit to the south. About four or five kilometres from our artillerymen I could again see the Egyptian camp. Because our guns had fired for a long time and had given away their presence and position, it was clear it would only be a matter of time until they were encircled by the Egyptians.

I tried going back into the cloud and locating our force, but without success. Visibility was zero. These were horrible moments; there was no way I could make it inside that cloud, and I knew for sure that if I left them there our boys would be wiped out.

Though we were in enemy territory and next to a large Egyptian camp – which was surely busy looking for our force – I decided as a last resort to descend three or four metres and turn on the Sea Stallion's great lights to search the area.

When the helicopter had gone a few metres above the ground with full illumination I asked the artillery commander to fire flares.

At first – nothing, but after tense seconds there were haloes of light inside the cloud, one after the other. We turned in their direction. My flight engineer was calling out the numbers on the electronic height indicator. There was no need to hear the numbers; as the height dropped his voice rose.

With the aid of smudge pots on the ground I was able to land the helicopter close to the artillerymen. But our troubles were not yet over.

I decided it would be better not to send the second helicopter into the cloud, but to try and load both cannons into my chopper, though such a thing was known to be virtually impossible.

The first cannon was placed inside with great difficulty and effort because the helicopter's winches had broken down. Afterwards we found that the cannon had been put in backwards; as a result there was little room for personnel, never mind the second cannon. Time was running out. Moving everyone back from the helicopter, I took off towards a nearby defilade and landed on the edge at a very steep angle; the nose was pointed into the depression while the belly rested flat on the ground.

The artillerymen moved the second cannon towards the nose-down helicopter and slid it inside. It crossed barrels with the first gun, while part of its body remained extended outside. Slowly and gently, I closed the ramp door to push the cannon inside. It fit. The gunners scrambled inside, the door closed and we took off without delay, getting away under the nose of the Egyptians.

On the way home we weren't spared problems. The stay on the mountain had consumed a lot of fuel, giving us something to worry about. The fuel pump broke down, though the dials worried me much more. We were busy with estimates the whole way home – would there be enough fuel, or wouldn't there? We took off overweight, with two cannons instead of one. The whole way I was thinking that the helicopter had to burn fuel or it wouldn't fly; here it was burning fuel and flying. Was there any other way? We kept flying and made it home.

The real reward came when we landed. A lieutenant colonel from the artillery came over and said, 'When the boys saw the cloud and heard about the helicopter's problems they were a little worried. But I knew you wouldn't leave us out there.'

Chapter 23
EJECTING INTO THE SEA OFF BEIRUT

At the height of the Yom Kippur War, during an attack against a Syrian airfield, the Phantom flown by Captain (Res) M was hit. With no chance of landing safely back in Israel, M and his navigator parachuted into the sea off Beirut.

I don't really like all those hot-shot stories about the heroism of our brave pilots, how we're so great and powerful and awesome, and always fearlessly defeating the enemy. It's not that all these stories are untrue; it's just that if there's any heroism in our war in the air there's nothing to wave the flag about. Our war is tough and fraught with danger, and the next one will be even tougher and more dangerous. You don't always win at war without paying a price; sometimes our planes are hit. And that's why, of all things, I want to tell a story about bailing out, the final story of Phantom No. 18.

From the beginning I saw that this sortie had started off on the wrong foot. It was 13 October and, in addition, it was the sabbath. They had woken me up in the middle of the night and informed me that the next day I was to lead one of the two formations earmarked to attack the Damascus-Mazzah airfield in the heart of the Damascus basin. This field was located smack in the middle of an area considered the hottest in terms of threats against our aircraft; it was surrounded by batteries of anti-aircraft missiles of all sizes. The Syrians considered Damascus-Mazzah to be of high strategic importance; its proximity to the front enabled the MiG-17s based there to take off and rocket our forces within the shortest of times and return immediately to a highly defended zone. So it was decided to attack the MiGs while they were still on the ground, to destroy them before they could take off. To do this we would have to go into the hell of the Damascus basin and up against the missile batteries and anti-aircraft guns. And therein lay the problem. In those days the ack-ack guns were considered our greatest danger – a good many losses were attributed to them, with aircraft being hit by gunfire while trying to avoid the missiles; the missiles we felt we could deal with, especially if we saw them in time.

We go out to the aircraft. Because the strike is planned for the early morning it's still pitch dark. I'm to fly this sortie with D, a senior and very experienced navigator. There are problems from the start. One aircraft breaks down; we're given a half-hour postponement, but in the end we take off.

The formation ahead of us had left a few minutes before. We fly behind it, first north and then east. And as we turn – whammo – a surprise. The sun has just now risen, large and bright, and it fills the whole horizon with a blinding brilliance. We look eastward – no chance; it's impossible to see a thing in this direction. We won't see anything coming from the east until it's already hit us.

The first formation decides to call it off and turns back. I decide to go on, taking the necessary precautions against any unpleasant surprise from the east. I concentrate on flying and manoeuvre sharply against any ack-ack fire. In the rear cockpit, D concentrates on the navigation and the attack plan.

Now there's ack-ack fire. Lots. Looking up ahead it seems the whole horizon is firing upwards, but maybe this is because the sun is rising and is glaring to the eye.

We arrive on target. I get set up and go in. I'm still worried and do what I have to against the ack-ack. Still can't see any missiles in the air. I turn – this is the heart of the Damascus basin, the area thickest with threats. Really murderous anti-aircraft fire, but still no missiles.

At some point a number of missiles begin to fly, but they still seem to pose no danger. I'm astounded the whole time. I try to avoid the ack-ack but it follows me stubbornly, one step behind, and I'm thinking, How can it be that I'm not being hit? I can't understand.

115

We go in for a pass. Here there are a few seconds of stable flight where I must concentrate on adjusting the bomb trigger. I get it in place, press the release, feel the bombs underneath disengaging and departing and then – whammo! I feel the aircraft take a hard knock. I've sustained a direct hit, apparently from a 57mm ack-ack shell.

Due to the hit, the missiles under my wing ignite. My navigator feels a jolt, sees the flash of the departing missiles and says, 'We're hit; we've got a fire in the left wing.' I see the missiles way out in front and realize what's confused him. 'It's okay,' I calm him, 'so far it's only our missiles.' At this point there's still no time to check the airplane, because off to the side are two missiles coming straight at our stricken Phantom. This time it seems sure: these missiles are right on target.

Right now the aircraft is at medium altitude and good speed. Hit or not, I don't plan on being struck by one of these missiles. I deal with the first one, which doesn't hit. According to D's instructions from the rear cockpit, I turn my attention to the other one; this, too, does no damage. Now I have a few seconds and can check the airplane over to see who and what's been hit.

First I check myself. I'm okay; haven't been hurt. The aircraft is also responding as it should. There are nevertheless some warning lights; the engines are stuck at full power, with no response from the throttles; the fuel indicators are moving at high speed. Other than this the aircraft is fully controllable. My first conclusion; I'm still on top of the situation and can get out of here. Afterwards we'll see. Meanwhile some more missiles pass overhead but cause no damage. I drop down to low level to look at my shadow, and see that this shadow is very, very large, as if I'm dragging something behind me. Now my Number Two joins up and says, 'Watch out, you're on fire!'

We depart the danger zone. Ground control suggests a heading of two-two-zero. Home. But in the rear cockpit D determines, two-seven-zero – the shortest route to the sea.

This would turn out to be one of the most fateful decisions we would make.

Meanwhile the aircraft is still flying. It's burning, and the throttles don't respond, but we can fly and even gain a little altitude. Overall we're going to pass about five to ten miles south of Beirut. It looks all right. But we're already beginning to think that maybe this plane is a goner ...

The thought is quite shitty, as if they've hit me right in my ego. How can it be? I wasn't prepared for this. I try to think where I went wrong. As they say, I'm screwed; they've got me. I begin feeling that I won't be bringing this airplane back to a landing. Aircraft No. 18, the first airplane in the squadron to have a camera gunsight installed. I'm not bringing this aircraft back!

I gain altitude in case I have any more problems and have to get out fast. But all the time I'm hoping that somehow the fire will go out and I won't have to jump, and that somehow it'll be all right. Later I'll lower the wheels – it doesn't matter – I'll shut down the engines and come in for a forced landing. I even try to coax the crews in the aircraft around us: 'So, the fire's going out, right? It's going out, isn't it?' 'Negative,' they answer, 'it doesn't look good from here. Not good.' And Number Two informs me, 'One, you're on fire. You can go a little farther, but get ready to jump.'

I look down – about half a minute to the coast. Meanwhile there are no signs in the cockpit of any fire. It's not hot and the controls are working. Can't see any fire from the cockpit; maybe everything will be okay in the end.

But now, just before crossing the coast, the controls freeze up. Actually they're not frozen; the stick just goes soft like butter and has no effect. And meanwhile the aircraft keeps flying straight and in a gentle climb.

And then they tell me, 'That's it! Jump!' I look down – the coastline is already near. I radio back. 'Three, can I wait a little longer?' At least to make it to the sea. 'Negative,' he answers. 'Negative! Jump!' And then someone else comes over the radio. 'Jump! Jump! Jump!'

I ask my navigator, 'Well, D, do we jump?' He says okay, that he's ready. I pull the levers.

How it hurts to leave the airplane. The whole time I had been thinking, What can I do to save it? Shut down an engine? I didn't even know what was burning. Such a shame. Here you are, getting ready to throw away an airplane – and in 1973 every Phantom was worth more than its weight in gold.

I close my eyes during the ejection procedure; I think it's safer. While D is already a veteran 'parachutist', this is the

117

first time in my life I'm ejecting. A pull on the lever, a few seconds of noise and tumult and all sorts of things, and suddenly the parachute opens and all around there's this kind of quiet. Altitude: 12,000 feet. Cold. It takes a long time to descend from this height – about twelve minutes in the air. It's ten minutes to six, and outside dawns a cool morning.

In the air, D shouts for me to try and pull myself west, out to sea. I try pulling all kinds of shroud lines; the canopy does a few rolls to the right, and afterwards a few rolls to the left. And meanwhile I see I'm going to come down on land near the highway south of Beirut. All kinds of thoughts go quickly through my head: What kind of people are waiting for me down there? The Lebanese Army? PLO? What kind of people are they?

We take a good look around, searching for the direction we'll be able to get away in. All told, the sea is close enough, and so are our forces. I also think a little about home, the wife, the kids. It wouldn't be right if we got ourselves caught right now. Yes, there's lots of time to think as we fall from Angels 12.

At 3000 feet there are a few wisps of cloud and, as we're crossing through this altitude, an easterly wind suddenly and miraculously appears and takes us out to sea. The further out we are, the more chance we have of being rescued.

Meanwhile people begin gathering on the highway across from us. A jeep with a machine-gun appears and opens fire. Others are shooting as well. I was never an infantryman, and this fire looks murderous. And here, a boat leaves the beach and speeds towards our estimated landing spot. It doesn't look good. But our aircraft are circling above, and now they're coming down on this boat, and also on those firing from shore, and things are looking up a little. It's a wonderful feeling, knowing your friends up above are now doing all they can to make sure you get home safely.

We land in the water and climb aboard our survival rafts. (In the coming days they would laugh a lot back at the squadron over the fact that, in the end, I had landed west of D despite his having been an experienced parachutist.) We sit in the rafts, waiting for the helicopter that will come and rescue us. An hour goes by before it arrives, picks us up and cruises south.

Once in the helicopter the events resurface. You say to

yourself, An aircraft is gone; was it all necessary? Did I have to go in there? Okay, there was the sun, and we had to alter the plan a little. But did we have to force the thing? I'm convinced a leader has to stick to his mission – though not if it's futile or the price is too steep. But he has to try to the best of his ability. We specifically went there to save our boys in the Golan who were getting screwed time after time by those MiG-17s. We had to stop them. True, it was dangerous; war is dangerous. In the infantry, men charge, and sometimes there are casualties. What is it they say? 'This won't happen to a Jew in New York.' But I was there, and it happened to me. I bought it.

This sortie, at least for me, was marked by extremes between the various stages, starting in the early morning at the squadron – still dark. Sitting in the lounge, drinking coffee and, pow! an hour later I find myself all over the place – fire, missiles, bailing out. And afterwards, another hour in the cold water.

I returned to the squadron and was grounded due to a leg injury I had suffered while ejecting. I sat at the squadron while others flew and fought. After a week I could no longer stand this; I went to the squadron leader and informed him that this was it, the next day I was flying.

At least on paper the story of bailing out was finished.

Chapter 24
WITH KATZ TO TANTA

*On the afternoon of Saturday 24 July 1982, an Israeli
Phantom was hit during a strike against Syrian SA-8 missile
batteries in Lebanon's Beka'a Valley. The navigator, Major
Aharon Katz, was killed. Brigadier General Asher Snir,
author of this chapter, had gone with Katz to attack the Tanta
air base in Egypt during the Yom Kippur War.*

For twelve years Phantom crews had been struggling against
Soviet-made SAM surface-to-air missile arrays. It was a
continuous battle between our best and their best, a battle
full of blood and losses on both sides, a key battle that
neither we nor they could circumvent.

On a Saturday afternoon, 24 July 1982, after they had
routed the SA-6 and -9 missiles, the Phantoms declared war
on the new SA-8 batteries, whose appearance marked their
world debut. When the sun went down three of the batteries
lay smashed and burnt. But this time things didn't end so
smoothly: one Phantom was downed in the Beka'a. Its crew
ejected, but Aharon Katz was dead when he hit the ground.
A little bit of all of us died with him, a wise, pure, strong,
special and memorable man.

This is the story of one flight with him in October of 1973.
It was an unforgettable flight, not only because of what
happened, but because of a very difficult hour and a half we
were together in an extraordinary spiritual struggle. When we

landed, we knew that we had needed everything between us for the flight to end as it did.

The setting was the Nile delta, the western part of a triangle with the Rosetta and Damietta. It was 15 October 1973, the middle of the Yom Kippur War. The people involved were twenty-four pilots and navigators from the Bat Squadron, riding a dozen Phantoms. The mission: attacking the Egyptian air base at Tanta. We were to show up in two pairs and two quartets.

I can't recall the exact sequence of events, but I remember an especially difficult briefing for a large formation that would have to be particularly well co-ordinated. Before us was a complex and deep penetration raid against a full array of opposition: anti-aircraft guns, missiles, MiGs – and a long way home. Nevertheless the briefing was hurried and the heart slowly filled with the worst feeling a fighter pilot could have: we weren't fully prepared. To a certain extent this was balanced out by the knowledge that the crews were the cream of the crop, that I would be leading once again with Katz, and that I had something going for me in the rear cockpit that would, no matter what, be sound, correct, on time and faultless. Katz was head and shoulders above the rest, among other things because he knew; he knew everything he had to, the whole kit and caboodle. As soon as we moved up to this complicated airplane, with its six main weapon systems and all the different possibilities and complex combinations, Katz stood out from the rest, a tall second lieutenant with a knitted skullcap and laughing, light blue eyes, who knew his stuff better than all of us.

When you flew with him you were free from all the minor distractions. What Katz said, you did, because his special wisdom was the wisdom of action, the wisdom of truth and not of strutting one's stuff.

You sat in the briefing and heard the complicated order of take-off and the management of communications, taxiing and the rest. You glanced at the maps and saw there would be some very difficult navigation – and an execution that was even more difficult. And you wanted to sit for just five minutes with your eyes closed, imagining the flight: the various situations, where to pay attention to what, what to navigate by, where the missiles would come from and when and where the MiGs would come; to see with your eyes closed the delta rolling beneath you at 100 feet and 550 knots, with the trees, power-lines and pylons flying by; in short, to think about the ten minutes that would determine everything. But there was no time. Hurry up, hurry up. And the aircraft were still undergoing final preparations; some would be ready only once we were getting hooked up in the cockpits. And you would go out with the feeling that, in order to prevent a twenty-minute delay, there would be a loss in performance and safety.

I go out with Katz to Phantom No. 119. Hands full of maps, quick guides for the complicated switches, photos of the targets, gunsight camera and helmet. Katz is also holding a stack of papers I didn't manage to organize properly because of the rush. I'll take them from him while taxiing, in the order they're supposed to appear, with all the critical information noted and emphasis on the check points and all the possible contingencies taken into account. (Katz writes every word twice, his pen running two times over the same lines. I will never ask him why he does this or where the habit comes from.) The two of us go over the aircraft manual and the aircraft itself, always the right thing to do, but now especially so. We're tired and the mechanics are tired, the work was rushed, the aircraft is not completely ready and now there's psychological pressure on the ground crews due to our mere presence.

We check the Vulcan gun and the radar, the large air intakes and the landing gear. We go over the clusters of green bombs and the missiles (old habits, but they're not overlooked during the rush; it doesn't matter how pressed you are for time, there are always a few seconds to take the cuff of your overalls and polish the glass nose of the green and venomous Sidewinder missile so it will 'see' things well and from far away); check the black exhaust pipes, the fuel tanks and plumbing of the afterburner; go over the wing's control surfaces and the tall tail with its red arrow and bat insignia.

We get in and buckle up in No. 119 and hook up to the oxygen and intercom.

'Katz, can you hear me?'

'Five by five.'

'Me, too. Ejection light?'

'On.'

It's a ritual that transforms our personal communication into something electronic. You don't see faces, you don't see moving lips; afterwards the dark visor comes down and you don't see eyes.

Turn on the great engines, start up the electrical system, switch off the warning lamps (aside from the last two which go out only on the runway); down below they've finished the final preparations and we head out to the runway. We taxi and during this time Katz, as expected, finishes organizing my paperwork and passes up the maps, which are already marked for zones protected by missiles and gone over for time co-ordinates, speeds, headings, landmarks and fuel computations. Once again I imagine the route, the points we'll have to find, from where we'll get the missile lock-on and from which nearby fields we might be jumped by their MiG patrols. Meanwhile the radar screen flickers green as Katz checks the large appliance in the black nose. Around us, our quartet gather with their compressors shrieking: Yoel and Ilan Fine, Dudu and Yaron, Dudik and Yitzhak. Omri's foursome gathers on the second runway and in front of both of us the pairs of Tzivikele and Arnon straighten out and take off with a bone-rattling roar.

Now we straighten out, run up the engines from a shriek to outright thunder and hear over the radio that Omri's quartet is taking off.

'Time,' says Katz, 'three, two, one, go.' Full afterburners and we're on our way.

We join up into fours on the long sea leg westward (a common mistake in geographical orientation; Egypt is west of Israel and not south). Once more Katz goes over the fuel computations; there's still a lot, but we know that over target, and after bombing, fuel will be the most important factor. Around us the great, dusky Phantoms loaded with bombs and fuel and exhaling black braids of smoke. We can't see the coast because of the distance and height, but we know from the inertial navigation system and time that on the left are Gaza, Rafiah and El Arish, and afterwards Bardawil, Port Said, the Manzala Marshes and Damietta estuary. In another moment we'll turn south and charge in from the north and into the delta.

We accelerate and sink down towards the sea; this is the place to say that spread out around the airfield are three

SA-3 batteries, which we already checked on a previous flight (they looked just fine) and another two of the SA-2, which in a flat area like the delta are a serious matter at all altitudes: early detection could be tragic. But so far things are quiet and everything's okay, except that the sea behind us looks like a flotilla of torpedoes had just passed by, covered with spray and steam.

A little before we are to cross the coastline I look back; someone's leaving Omri's quartet – fuel transfer problem – and we cross the coast as a pair, a threesome and a foursome staggered to the right. Two in the formation are not in place because we have to run along the same line. It's important to point out that for a straight bombing run, an error of a mile, or even two, means problems, but is no tragedy. In contrast, anyone who flies a bombing run against anti-aircraft guns has to be very precise with his navigation or the whole run will go for naught.

We cross the enemy coast roughly where we planned. There's a low, diagonal sand bar, a salt-water marsh called Lake Burlus and lots of islets and bunches of reeds. You still don't know where you are – is this an island or just mud? The second coastline comes right away and it, too, is wishy-washy; and you know that if you haven't pinpointed your position by the time you reach the delta farmland, you certainly won't be able to do it there. You have to decide. Now.

We can't identify our precise position, but deep down the feeling grows that we're too far left, even though we're the ones on the right. The distance between the coastal sand bars, maybe a larger island, part of a hill in the corner of your eye, and other such trivia, and I correct to the right according to Katz's and my intuition that this is it. Which is to say, exactly how not to navigate. But the two of us have considerable experience and I have been here once or twice before. A bank to the right and that's it.

Tension now in the two cockpits. They had come up with co-ordinates for the final, fateful leg from a railway junction. They had come up with it and we had no time to switch this to something clearer. Now, instead of concentrating on a flight over enemy territory, we have to deal with tough and bothersome navigation. Why the hell a railway line? I mean, anyone knows that all the delta's features – canals, roads, railways – look alike from 100 feet since they're all between tall rows of trees; and the entire delta is full of them, like the strands in a fisherman's net. But you can find your way in the delta by the curves and bridges of the Damietta and Rosetta, and according to big cities with industry. There are also a large number of towns and villages and you see smokestacks and factories. But we've already made up our minds and there's nothing more we can do – in a little while the missiles will be flying.

The place comes up and the warning screen fills; lines of light sprouting and getting longer, SA-2s and SA-3s and warning chirps of all types flow one on top of the other. Together, Katz and I had checked the many switches while still over the sea and we double-checked; but we now send a final glance at the green and orange lights because we'll have to be ready for the missiles and for that miserable railway junction – if it ever shows up, because its time has already come.

To our surprise we hit the crossroads with utmost precision and Katz says, this is the junction: take this and this direction; there's this much longer to go till pulling; turn, turn. We turn towards the final leg. I rock wings for my formation – a sign to speed up – and open my throttles full; the speed indicator rises to 560–570 knots.

Katz says, 'Everyone's clean; everyone's in place.' Omri's trio is ahead and to the left and I know he'll be able to deal with being a little to the side. I also know it won't be a good bombing run with the cluster bombs on the field and it appears the hit will be forward and to the left – south and east of the runways and anti-aircraft. And we'll also have to contend with active ack-ack.

The electronic warning instrument changes pitch and Katz says, 'Watch out, hot warning at 12 o'clock,' and some other technical things. He is speaking quickly and in something of a high voice. No worry or fear; the verbal pipeline is simply too narrow for the overflow of the thought process and for the speed at which events are unfolding. I know him from dozens of operational flights together, a few of them especially dicey – and I listen and absorb. (Katz was brave. True bravery, not ignorance, but rather wisdom and precise knowledge of where he was heading. Just the week before, it had been necessary to go over the Syrian heights at medium altitude to draw some missiles away from a buddy caught at low speed on the way to Damascus. Katz had said, 'No problem,' without hesitation or a change in his voice. A number of years later I was to see his short diary from that war. On that event he wrote: 'Terrific fear; I never thought I'd get out of that one alive.')

A cloud of white explodes on the horizon and flowers into a mushroom. As expected, the missiles begin to fly: three distant 'telephone poles' rise up slowly, misleading anyone unfamiliar with them. We watch them with half an eye (the remaining eye and a half fly the Phantom at a height of 100 feet, almost 300 metres per second, above the green patch-work of the delta), and look for the downward arc that will tell us whether they're coming towards us. An SA-3 missile always rises straight up, until it separates from its booster and its steering mechanism is freed, and you have to watch out. The seconds go by and the trio is still climbing. Bon voyage; we have to ignore them.

The second bombing pair, which belongs to Tzvikele and is coming from the east, reports on the radio about missiles and MiGs over the field and that they're waging a dogfight or two, as long as their fuel allows. Meanwhile we're about to pull. There's not much time, and we're set up so that Livne and Sofer, Omri's rightmost crew, are in front of me and a little to the left. And everyone is on the deck, licking the weeds.

Katz says, 'Everyone's all right. Two minutes to pull.'

The next thing that comes up is two SA-3 missiles, leaving the horizon directly ahead and flying straight for us like beams of light. But it's already 15 October. The war is ten days old and we know exactly what to do. We pull up a bit so there will be room for a good break; healthy speed and half burner; everyone with me, well set up and waiting to see what will happen. The crews quickly see that the missiles are not going after them, but the missiles are still running in my general direction and to the left. After super-low flight and having locked on to a mosque or antenna, the first one hits a village with an awful explosion two or three kilometres ahead. Just as we feel 'our missile' has exploded and is gone, I see the second one catch Livne and Sofer's Phantom, ahead and to the left, blowing up very close on the right.

Livne pulls in a hard climbing turn to the right, leaving a

light trail of leaking fuel or smoke in the sky, and dropping everything he had hanging – fuel tanks, bombs and racks – and heads north towards the sea at an altitude of 2000 or 3000 feet. I have a hard choice to make: Livne is badly damaged and barely flying, 350 kilometres from home and needing all the help he can get. Against this, only six of us are left to put our sights on the main target. Escort Livne or not? Katz says nothing. He doesn't burden me with trivia or melodrama; he knows my dilemma very well and knows he must help out, and not hinder. The seconds go by in silence. It's impossible to stop for a moment and deliberate; there are 600 knots on the gauge. Three hundred metres per second, fast as a bullet above the checkerboard delta and I decide. I half-say, half-ask over the intercom, 'We'll try to catch up with him on the way out.' Ten years between us. I'm the older. I wait to hear what he'll say. Katz says, 'Fine,' and I thankfully blot out the dilemma – for now.

What Katz had gone through, weighing morality as a human being and as a soldier, we've all gone through. He even called me by name so I'd know the matter was personal. The whole thing, three to five seconds of a question with no answer, and our orientation is back on the target beyond the black nose.

'Ten seconds to pull,' says Katz. 'Two, Three and Four are all right.' I look again. Yoel, Dudu and Dudik, right in place, three dark Phantoms, huge and radiating power. Twenty-five tons of momentum that won't be stopped. There's no black smoke from the engines; everyone's already on afterburner and the speed gauge creeps to 610, 620 knots.

Meanwhile, over with Livne the silence tells of bad news from the rear cockpit; fire warning lights and a crunching noise from the engines. For a minute or two he flies like this, then all the hydraulics go, the elevators jam in the full-up position and the stricken Phantom jumps upwards out of control. Livne and Sofer are out, on parachutes, and none of us can help. We hear no more from them. (Livne was taken captive and came back; young Sofer was mortally wounded inside the aircraft and was apparently dead before he hit the ground. Brave and fair and twenty years old.)

'Get ready to pull,' says Katz. 'Pull!' There is merriment in his voice, the exaltation of one facing the height of battle and gratefully accepting it. It's correct to place force against force, speed against fire, wisdom against wisdom. Katz loves people. If you have seconds in which to think, you have to ask where they have come from. The two of us alone are going to fling some two tons of bombs on a field below, and you wonder how love for man and joy of battle can reconcile themselves, how this man has found himself leading a quartet of Phantoms to kill and destroy. He's a wonder of wonders of the Land of Israel, which he loves with a yearning. Maybe this, too, is the answer.

Full afterburners, 630 knots. The nose is in the sky, the delta sinks away and the horizon suddenly widens. The view is important, but not as important as the SA-3 battery we've passed right over. Its anti-aircraft is alert and cocked, firing at us with every piece. Another penalty of the rush to head out; there was no time to move the route and now we're stuck with our luck against theirs. This time our speed tips the scales and we all come out of the mushroom carpet without a scratch.

Omri's pair gets ready to go in ahead and to the left, and in a moment we will too. The Tanta field stretches out below on the left side. A last glance around to look for the MiGs, which are certainly on patrol here. It's clear above and to the sides and also outside the turn; no MiGs and no missiles. My four are okay and so is Omri's pair. We're at 10,000 feet and we'll continue to pick up speed from the momentum. The anti-aircraft fire is thick and powerful, but lower than us. And all of us, almost together, wheel around and go in. Katz says so far everything's clear. My head is in the purple sights. Katz has already locked the radar on the ground echo and is ready to keep up on this manually if the radar lock should come undone for some reason. He calls out the descending height. The speed, which dropped in the steep climb, increases once more and within seconds we've made it back to 550 knots. Lined up well, with everything we've got, so we won't disappoint anyone. A strong press on the trigger. A chirp from the computer, a series of successive shocks from the wings as the bombs depart and out.

We head out north and I turn left sharply, to the west, in order to see the second pair in their pass and, especially, what's happening behind them. Katz says everyone's clean and Dudik, who's last, is indeed out to the north and he seems clean.

Back to Yoel and Fine, our Number Two, and we make two turns to bring them line abreast with us and quickly check what's going on behind. This time they're there: two MiG-21s sitting on Yoel at missile range. A warning over the radio, he breaks, with us alongside. While breaking, my left hand finds its way to the low-mounted armament panel and turns the switches to air-to-air. Yoel is in a hard break to the south and left of us at a height of two or three thousand feet and the two MiGs to his rear have already closed in to gun range. We get rid of everything hanging on our Phantom with one strong press of the 'panic button'. The afterburners are open wide and with a barrel roll we get right in to gun range behind the two MiGs. Katz is ready, with his head backwards to see that no more MiGs are coming from the same direction. Yoel meanwhile breaks from side to side in a general northerly direction, and the closer and more threatening MiG loses some of its geometrical advantage.

The second one sees us coming and breaks hard up and to the right. I threaten him a little more so he'll keep breaking and head away. The MiG's silhouette extends to its full length and it moves away to the side and rear. Good. At least we'll be rid of him for a while, and we reverse our turn to the left and go back to the lead MiG, this time for the kill, in close and with cannon.

The powerful Phantom easily closes in with its roaring, red-hot afterburners. Yoel breaks from side to side and the MiG is losing its advantage, though it's still there in the rear still threatening. The fuel is running out on the gauge like blood and we have to hurry. The two throttles are full forward and the sights are coming up on the line of flight. Not too fast; don't get uptight, don't think about Yoel and Fine being in the balance, don't make a mistake. Stay quiet, be professional; think about the lines of flight and the range, about the closing speed and the rate of turn.

I spit into the intercom, 'Look behind, Katz, my head's in the sights.' Katz is ready with his head looking back. Up ahead the height of all drama: range diminishing to close combat, the Egyptian MiG and the Phantom; friends on the scales between life and death. And Katz turns to the rear, where it's his job to look back on the smoking field getting farther away; at the brown and dusty horizon; into the afternoon skies to the south; at the patchwork of yellow and green below. 'All clear,' says Katz. 'Also visual contact with the one you let go and he's far off and poses no danger.'

Meanwhile Yoel forces the MiG to raise its nose into our sights, long and speckled. Two hundred and eighty metres and closing, the sights are on the wingroot; I press the trigger. A second-long howl from the Vulcan cannon and the air between the sights and the MiG is filled with rushing fireflies. The MiG is finished: the left wing catches fire, the fuselage explodes, the right wing blows off. I pull up and over with a lowered wing so Katz will see what we did to him. Quick instructions for Yoel to close his burners, reverse his turn and straighten out to the north, and again we're in a line abreast, sinking towards the delta. Home. Behind us the MiG's fuselage spins to the ground, pulling behind it a yellow-red-black flame thirty or forty metres long. To the side the Egyptian is hanging from his parachute. There are already no fuel reserves ... northward, northward, as far as possible.

'The second one's coming back,' says Katz over the radio so we'll all see and hear. We spread out a little wider, climb a bit and look back. We don't have the fuel for a fight but we're armed and set up enough so that with one turn of 90 degrees we'll be able to lay him to rest with his forefathers if he really does try to come in. The Egyptian is very careful, certainly shaken up like he should be, and doesn't come in. Then Katz says, 'Watch out, he's launched. Quite far off.' The MiG's Atoll missile flies for a kilometre and its engine then flames out. One eye on the missile, the other on the MiG. One eye on the checkerboard ground, the other on Yoel's Phantom. The missile slowly, slowly, slowly loses stability and begins to weave between us like a drunken snake.

The ground starts turning yellow and the MiG disappears and we're once more over Lake Burlus, going very easy on the engines, a lot slower than we'd like. It's no small relief when you're over the sea, but only in retrospect, because in the meantime I'm looking for Dudu and Dudik on the radio and I simply cannot find them. Despite this the radio says Omri's taken a close missile explosion and is flying home without ailerons. The radio also says they're calling Livne and Sofer on the emergency channel and there's no answer. Might be that I've lost half a formation. Turn to the east towards our far-off home and pull Yoel into a climb to high altitude because there's no more fuel for flying low.

Calling and calling to Three and Four on all the channels; going into clouds at 30,000 feet and hiding inside them, really short on fuel. Off Port Said, Dudu and Dudik come over the radio. A great relief that, this time, everyone with me is all right.

A long flight home at altitude. The base commander in the distant command bunker knows where we've been and how things look. He asks, 'Everything okay by you?' 'Affirmative, affirmative,' I answer and by Port Said you can hear the relief in the short 'Roger' with which he replies.

The various formations return home in a glide and gather for landing. Everyone expects us. We owe ourselves something else, a buzz and a victory roll. We close in at altitude until Ashdod and lower the heavy black nose towards our base, which is between Philistia and Judea. We descend, straighten out in front of the squadron building, and afterwards, at no altitude and with open burners, the three of us, as one, storm above the boys, thrusting the nose into the skies and being carried aloft with a series of quick rolls so there will be no doubt that in this fight we were the winners.

September, 1981. I'm still in uniform. I've been appointed base commander. A job for a general. Katz, who's also still in uniform, comes by to offer congratulations. I remain a little anxious about the responsibility. There are still ten years between us; it's already unimportant. 'Katz,' I say, with doubt in my laughter, 'when it was really tough I was used to having you a metre and a half behind me. What's going to happen now?'

'This isn't so bad,' Katz laughs with blue eyes at six-foot-three. 'When it gets really tough, call me.'

And so, Katz, my boy, this still holds for me. Rest in peace in the meantime. If it really gets tough we'll call you. And you'll come.

Chapter 25
MY MOST DIFFICULT MISSION

During the first week of the Yom Kippur War, a formation of Phantoms went out to attack the airbase at Mansura, in Egypt's Nile delta. Colonel R's aircraft was caught in an ambush by Egyptian MiGs. R and the navigator, the late Yitzhak Baram, were able to get out of the trap, but experienced one of the war's most difficult sorties.

I have to tell the story of this flight very slowly and with a lot of concentration. It was a very difficult flight, and unique. I call it the toughest sortie of my life.

Its beginnings were on 11 October, when my squadron took part in an attack on the Benha airfield in the Nile delta. The aircraft were caught on the way back by MiGs from six o'clock. A tough dogfight ensued and a number of MiGs were shot down, as were two of our Phantoms. This fight left a bitter taste with the squadron.

On the morning of the 14th a formation from the squadron went to Mansura, also in the Nile delta. It was clear that this was going to be a tough raid. Even very tough. The Mansura field was deep in the delta and was protected by batteries of SA-2 and -3 missiles. MiGs were expected in the target zone and the chances we would take them by surprise were slim.

The first navigation leg was made over the sea. My navigator was the late Yitzhak Baram, who was killed a year later in an accident. We flew and strained our eyes in an effort to locate threats such as MiGs or missiles. So far, everything was quiet.

But ground control came on even before we crossed the coastline. 'Watch out, there are MiGs above your target.'

'Got it,' our leader answered and to the formation he added, 'continuing as normal.'

Okay; now there were both missiles and MiGs. The tension in every cockpit increased.

The delta navigation leg was long. We were flying at very low altitude, so low that once or twice we had to pull up in order to pass over the great high-tension lines stretched across the area. We would have to remember these power-lines on the way back. We neared the target and the controller once more warned us about the MiGs. There was no doubt that there would be no element of surprise here. We would have to execute the raid as quickly as possible; if we remained at altitude for a few seconds too many the missile batteries would catch us. And if they couldn't, the MiGs would. Nor was there all that much fuel for roughing it up.

We arrive and pull over Mansura. We take a good look around; there's still no visual contact with enemy aircraft, but we can see MiG droptanks spinning towards the ground – which is to say that MiGs are above us. They've seen our Phantoms and are now getting set up to come in on the formation.

It's a tough decision: should you show your tail to the MiGs and dive on the target? (During the aiming phase you fly for a moment without manoeuvring and it's easy for them to get set up on you. Just three days before two aircraft had gone down after getting caught from behind by MiGs.) Or should you emergency-dump all your ordnance and try to get away before it's too late? (But then, why bother to make this long and dangerous flight?)

Number Two and I decide to go on. We hope the MiGs won't be able to launch any missiles until bomb release. Afterwards we'll see. We go in and bomb the runway; another second and large mushrooms of smoke rise exactly from where they're supposed to. Phase one has been executed well. Now we have to go over to phase two: getting home safely!

We exit with a hard break; we still don't see the MiGs but

133

we know they're somewhere in our rear. And here Number Four begins to shout that he's on fire. (Afterwards, in the debriefing, one of the pilots said that his first thought on hearing the shout was, Okay, so what do you want us to do? Bring a fire extinguisher?)

I turn towards Number Four; the Phantom doesn't seem to be burning. But there are two MiGs closing in from behind.

'Four, break hard left. They're sitting on you.'

Four breaks left, with me following in on the threatening MiGs. It's hard to get out from an absolute disadvantage by yourself; that's why we talk so much about defence and mutual assistance.

But why does Four think he's on fire? His navigator is new to the trade, a youngster really. He had had very few flights on this aircraft when the war broke out. Now, coming out of an attack, he hears shouts over the radio that there are MiGs and that they're firing. When he looks to the side he discovers wingtip vortices resulting from the high speed. He thinks it's smoke and informs the pilot. And right away comes the shout: I'm on fire.

I turn into the MiGs and drop some ordnance to clean up the aircraft. We're still not thinking in terms of a dogfight – more in terms of getting a partner out of a disadvantage. Indeed, the MiGs are giving up, and turning their attention to me while breaking away from Four, who straightens out and runs home – still convinced he's on fire.

The MiGs' break doesn't look too nice. It seems as if they've received a warning from someone. Which means there are more MiGs around. And indeed, Baram soon shouts, 'Break! They're sitting on us!' I break and look back: two MiGs; range, 600 to 700 metres. Two spumes of smoke suddenly depart the MiGs and run towards me. Air-to-air missiles!

I pull back on the stick a little more. The missiles miss and the MiGs pull ahead.

For a split second I hesitate on whether to do something about this pair of MiGs or break for home. And then Baram shouts for me to break once more, that another pair of MiGs is coming in. I don't know if this is the first pair, or if I'm up against six. At this point I've already broken hard twice; I'm low on speed and beginning to feel the pressure. I break a third time and my speed drops even more. And I don't have enough fuel to get into a dogfight.

'Number Three in trouble with MiGs,' I radio. I hope someone will come and get me out of here. I'm at very low altitude and see the MiGs behind me starting to get set up. I manoeuvre sharply.

'Are they still in the rear?' I ask Baram.

'Affirmative,' he answers.

'You sure?'

'Yes,' he says, 'and now they're firing.'

There are to be two especially difficult parts to this battle. The first will be when I realize that I'm alone above Mansura, in trouble with four and perhaps six MiGs, and that no one is about to come to my aid. No one; the rest of my formation is already far from the field. You're by yourself – sink or swim. The second difficult part was the turn. The lessons of Benha were still fresh in my mind; here, I apparently had what I needed to get out of trouble – good speed and I was well set up in a turn – but there was nothing else in my favour.

Okay, I've made up my mind. I'm going to try something else. Baram screams: 'Break! They're firing!' And here I pull up the nose sharply and look back to see what will happen.

The MiGs pull up after me. If they make it I'm finished. Right now I'm climbing vertically, with the speed dropping off. The MiGs are behind but they can't keep up; they break contact in the middle of their pull-up and call it quits. Now I raise my head: up above is the second pair, just waiting for me to fall to one side so they can come in on me. And of course I have to fall because my speed is already just about gone. This is what they mean by 'out of the frying pan and into the fire'.

The best pilot in the Air Force once said, 'When I'm at a total disadvantage, I pull manoeuvres that would keep even me from shooting myself down – if I could only get in behind myself.' A pretty wise statement and something I'm going to do right now. I'm up fairly high and now lower my nose in a completely vertical dive towards the ground.

At about the halfway point I know that if I don't pull out now I won't at all. I wait another second and pull on the stick with all my might, recovering at tree-top height. The MiGs are right behind, range about 1000 metres. They start setting up. Should I continue home at full power? The wheels in my head are spinning at top speed: my fuel is already well below the minimum required for a guaranteed return. I'll go on at full power, right on the deck; they'll have a very hard time aiming and hitting me. But a few miles ahead are the high-tension lines; I'll have to rise above them and then the MiGs will screw me. There's no choice; I'll have to turn to get them out in front.

I turn hard. The two MiGs are behind, and Baram occasionally shouts for me to break as they launch missiles and fire their cannons. And then I go back to the move I pulled before, suddenly raising the nose to 90 degrees, as hard as I can. Will they keep up?

This time, too, the MiGs can't hold on and they fall away before I do.

My fuel is already very low. While pulling out I decide I'll continue to attempt to break away till I hit half the amount I have now. If I can't break contact by then, I'll straighten out to the north and try to bail out over the sea at least. I already have my doubts about getting home with this amount of fuel.

I go completely vertical. The MiGs have fallen away. We look around: none of them is in a threatening position. I choose a clear piece of sky and lower my nose towards it in a vertical dive like before. I begin to pull back and straighten out with the tree tops. We don't see anyone to the rear and we decide in this case to speed home as low as possible. Baram constantly clears the tail.

I feel I have to say a few words about this guy, may he rest in peace; it was during this flight that I 'discovered' him. Before this I had thought he was just an average navigator, but here he was really outstanding. He was able to read the situation excellently; the whole time he would keep his eyes on the pair of MiGs I had no time for and he provided me with the correct flight directives. A number of times I did what he told me to, only afterwards seeing the MiGs, and I would tell myself, 'Aha! How right I was to have done that!' It's not too easy for a pilot to say, but I say it with all my heart: if Baram hadn't been with me out there I wouldn't have come back from Mansura. He simply provided the best I could ask for in the circumstances.

We're approaching the power lines. Baram clears me and I pull up for a moment and then go back down and again stick close to the ground. Fuel's running out. I shut down the afterburners; speed drops off a bit and then stabilizes. Engines at full dry. The main problem right now, the principal enemy, is the fuel situation.

We cross the coast towards home. Fuel's at a minimum. Start to climb. It's still impossible to take a homeward heading because we'll have to bypass the fortifications of Port Said, with their surface-to-air missiles. At any rate, a number of missiles are fired at us as we pass north of Port Said; they fall into the sea in mid-flight.

Where will we reach from here? Even Refidim is too far. I have 1000 pounds of fuel and there's only one possible place: Baluza, the narrow and short strip close by the road, right at the edge of their missile umbrella. I go over the radio: 'Number Three coming down at Baluza. Prepare the runway for landing.' I hope I'll find Baluza and that there'll be enough fuel.

Number Four suddenly comes over the radio. 'I'm also going to land at Baluza.'

Only one aircraft at a time can land at Baluza. Right now I'm down to 700 pounds and I won't make it anywhere else. It's Baluza or bail out. I tell this to Number Four. 'Okay,' he answers, 'I don't have much either. Whoever gets to Baluza first lands.'

He's got time to joke around. I inform him in the sternest terms to go to Refidim. He reconciles himself to this and makes it to Refidim for landing. I wouldn't have made it.

I call Baluza control tower. Someone answers in a weak voice: 'Hear you; where are you coming in from?' It seems he's not used to speaking with aircraft. Barely hear him. Baram and I look for the runway and with great effort find it and move into final approach. People and a vehicle can be seen next to the runway. And here, in the middle of final, the controller tells me, 'Go round, you can't land.' I'm not sure I have enough fuel, but what can you do? I open the throttles for five seconds and go round.

'What's wrong?' I ask and, to myself, I add that another moment and I'll have to bail out.

'You can't land that way,' the man in the tower tells me, 'because the wind is the wrong way.'

This is a bit much for my nerves right now. 'Imbecile!' I shout over the radio. 'For this you send me around? You just check and tell me whether the runway is clear for landing!'

137

'The runway is clear,' he says, 'but the wind is still coming the wrong way.'

My fuel right now is less than 300 pounds and from time to time the indicator shows empty. I straighten out again according to the procedures for a forced landing and expect to hear the engines quit. Right now nothing can prevent me from touching down on the runway.

Another five seconds; four, three and I'm down. I begin running along the landing strip. Its width is like a narrow road. I feel I'm drifting and that I'm going to go off the runway; I shut down the engines and ... catch the arresting cable while I'm still on the roadway. We did it.

I have never felt such a strong sense of relief as when we get out of our cockpits and hug.

Chapter 26
THIS TIME WE DID IT

At the height of the Yom Kippur War, after breaking the initial momentum of the Egyptian and Syrian armies, it was decided to destroy the Egyptian missile array. The operational goal was to restore Israel's air superiority in the skies of the Middle East. The job was given to one of the Phantom squadrons; the objective was attained, but at a heavy cost. The leader of the mission was Brigadier General A, then commander of the squadron.

At the opening of the Yom Kippur War dozens of missile batteries, completely overlapping one another, were dispersed along the length of the Suez Canal from Port Said in the north to the Gulf of Suez in the south. The batteries were a mixture of all kinds of missiles: SA-2s, -3s and -6s. The SA-6 had first appeared in the theatre a very short time before the war broke out and we still weren't totally familiar with them.

During the first stages of the war we tried to integrate strikes to subdue the missiles of both Egypt and Syria. These were interrupted by the urgent need to help our ground troops, and by the imbalance of forces – not in our favour. We went into action under limited conditions and, to a great extent, with our hands tied. The missile arrays cost us many losses and reduced the Air Force's strike capability. We penetrated, manoeuvred and attacked, but the missiles kept us from realizing our full potential.

After the initial containment phase of the war and with the beginning of the counterattack, we could organize an all-out effort to attain air superiority in the spirit of our Air Force tradition.

On 17 October, a forum of senior officers, led by the Air Force chief, gathered to appraise the situation and plan future strategy. At that point Egypt and Syria had already lost more than three hundred aircraft, and their opening momentum had been broken. Syria had been pushed back. Egypt was holding fast to the territory it had succeeded in occupying, but was unaware of our present plans for a counterattack and Canal crossing; and when the Egyptians saw signs of the crossing, they took it to be a limited action.

On our side fatigue was mounting, too: pressure to support the ground forces, and the difficulties and dangers of doing so, meant that a lot of us were going long periods without sleep; many aircraft were damaged and returned to service only after tireless effort by support personnel, and dozens more were hit, with their crews bailing out. Above all, the absence of lost friends weighed heavily upon us all.

After presenting the situation, Air Force GOC Benny Peled stated that it was necessary to begin the battle for air superiority. The chosen objective was a missile complex around Qantara, which would be the key to the battle.

The complex consisted of a mix of missiles, including SA-6s. The whole area was defended by additional batteries covering the west and south. Destroying the complex would open an aerial passageway for the entire northern Canal front, and allow air activity against the Egyptian Second Army, now on the eastern side of the Canal.

A force of Phantoms and Skyhawks was chosen to execute the mission, with my squadron in the lead. I went back to base, gathered my flight leaders and explained the situation. They were unanimous about the need to destroy the missile complex; the discussion was only about tactics. The leaders, pilots and navigators were busy all night preparing for the operation: maps, fuel considerations, distances, altitudes, intelligence.

I got to work on the make up of crews that would take part. Most had experience from the War of Attrition. This operation was to be the turning point in the air battle; destroying the missile system would not only free the skies over the northern Canal, it would prove the superiority of aircraft over missiles. So I needed to choose the most experienced among the crews – those who had demonstrated ability and cool heads under fire.

The list of participants was completed; we allowed them to get some sleep till sunrise.

Near the end of the briefing, tension begins to rise – a tension mixed with pride: the crews know they have been chosen to destroy a major part of the Egyptian air defence system, opening the way for additional operations that will completely take out the missiles.

After sunrise the base quakes from the roar of aircraft engines. All the planes are ready for take-off. When everything is set and the operation has been given the green light, we pull on to the runway and, one after the other, release our brakes. The heavy aircraft, loaded to the maximum with bombs and fuel, roll slowly for the first few metres, then build up speed and, one after the other, we are in the air.

I pull all eight aircraft together into an organized formation as we turn west towards the sea. In the background we hear the rest of the attack force grouping up from the various air bases and joining us in low flight over the water. The aircraft are spread along the length and breadth of our route – a great mass of speed, power and fire, rolling headlong at increasing velocity towards the strike zone.

The skies are bright and clear, to match the calm surface of the sea. Not a wave to be seen and the water looks like green glass. As we approach Egyptian shores, we stick closer to the water to prevent enemy radar from picking us up too early. This leg of the flight lasts about a quarter of an hour.

We haven't yet got over the rush of preparation and here we are nearing the point of penetration into enemy territory. A, the navigator sitting at the back, makes sure we're on course and carries out a basic check of the navigation and bombing systems. Another moment and we're in the battle arena. After a long radio silence I run a communication check and make sure everyone is in place. I exchange an 'off the record' word with A – and we are ready to go in.

At the last minute, I contact ground control to make sure there are no further instructions; I can take it that battle conditions fit the intelligence reports we were given ahead of time, and that the mission can run as planned.

We pass above our turning point and, at my sign (a wiggle of the wings) the giant formation begins to turn left towards the south. A light pull-up for the turn, look to the rear – I see the whole 'convoy', like a flock of iron birds coming in on their prey, straightening out to the south. We turn towards the Egyptian shore, to our right the Damietta Gulf, to our left Port Said. Between them, along the swamps of the delta, we prepare to cross the coast into Egyptian territory.

Radio silence continues. Tension mounts. There's a possibility at this point that the Egyptians will discover us and scramble their forces for a welcome. Here and there are signs that enemy radar is illuminating us. One quick sentence to cut the silence: 'Attention, we're crossing the coast in place and on time.' So far everything is going according to plan. Now we have to activate our diversion to suppress the Egyptian defences. I ask myself if they're in place and on time like we are, and if this is having any effect on the enemy defence array.

There's no time to dwell on nagging thoughts. The aircraft clings to the water and the speed picks up. I accelerate to close to Mach 1 and everyone follows. We're the opening formation, the trail blazers, and our success will determine the level of surprise and success of the overall mission. Ten seconds, five, here's the thin coastal strip with its row of upright white poles whose size testifies that these are ground-to-air missiles.

We knew about the missile array and thought we knew its exact position. As we pass over, and get a closer look, these turn out to be Egyptian fishing boats with thin, white sails standing vertical to the water. The optical illusion caused a few unnecessary heartbeats.

The shallow water slowly becomes muddy, and then turns to sandy ground. In every direction stretches infinite, flat, uniform and monotone sand.

Suddenly, as if by prearranged signal, everything comes to life. Our warning instruments begin flooding us with audio signals. This is it. The enemy's found us. It's late, but the sudden awakening suggests that they deliberately waited until the last moment before giving away the fact that they were on to us. Maybe they did discover us late, but it's still early enough to use their missiles. From here on everything goes at a dizzying speed. Have to think fast. Every second brings a new development and this is exactly where cool heads come in. Our responses are almost instinctive: action born of practice and experience.

The SA-6 is quite efficient and able to hit us at low altitudes as well. We realize that we have to stick to the ground as much as possible. But there's nowhere to hide because the terrain is too flat. We're flying at maximum speed, closer and closer to the ground – at this height it's possible to see the camel tracks. The problem is we won't be able to fly for long in these conditions.

A, my navigator, tries to estimate enemy range and intent. Meanwhile we continue to fly very low, our best protection – unless it turns out that we're right in the heart of the ambush envelope, then we'll have no choice but to rely on speed and manoeuvrability as we climb just before the bombing dive.

According to plan, our flight path would have us to the west of the missile complex, so that we'd be heading south and, with a left turn, we'd bomb the objective in an eastward dive. As luck would have it our flight path turns out to be between the target and the SA-6s; during our pull up and eastward turn, we'll leave the ambush behind us and have no way to watch it during the turn and eastward dive. We won't be able to use evasive manoeuvres. A real bitch, but there's no changing the course of the raid.

We stick to the ground and suddenly I hear R, who's leading the other four, announce over the radio, 'I'm hit!' That's all we need. I confer with A and together we decide to go on. R is definitely hit, but still flying. I look at the warning panel and see that once more we're being threatened from the same direction, from the right and slightly ahead. This time we're close to target and can already see a small protrusion on the flat surface. No doubt this is the ambush battery. I'm worried about R and look around for his aircraft, but the speed and altitude require my attention to remain within just a narrow angle.

I decide to stick to the ground. There's a ball of fire coming from that threatening point on the horizon. The flash telling you that a missile is coming your way is a constant spot on the canopy. And that's indeed what this is. The spot of fire grows in size, all the time remaining in the same place on the canopy. In front of it one can easily see the missile, whose flight path is right at us. If I decide to break or turn east towards our territory, the whole operation will be wasted. I decide to press on. Stick to the ground and hope. The missile tries to drop down after me but at the halfway point it hits the ground and explodes. Another missile comes right after it and this, too, explodes on the ground. A sigh of relief and we're already close to the pull-up point before the attack.

The sense of relief is cut short after a few seconds by a call over the radio. 'I'm hit!' I recognize the voice: Guri Palter, who's also in R's formation. Things are getting worse. I reconsider calling off the attack, but no, it's not right to give up. A gives encouragement. We can't fail this time. Even if it means losses. If we make it now, we've beaten the missiles. If we give in we've failed and the missiles have won.

A reminds me to pull up. We've reached the point. The radio is already flooded with calls, warnings, descriptions of R's and Guri's situations and directives from the far-off controller. I open the throttles and afterburners all the way forward to squeeze more power. The smack in my back tells me the afterburners are open; the aircraft accelerates and nothing will stop it. Sixty tons of steel, fuel and bombs at the speed of sound. Top speed and power, minimum height.

Right on the dot I pull back on the stick; the aircraft rears up 90 degrees towards the sky and momentum turns into a fast climb to altitude. We can't leave ourselves vulnerable – this is the most dangerous part, and all during the climb I'm thinking. Can't fly straight; at first upwards, afterwards a little to the sides and already I have to find the target. We have ten seconds. I look to the sides; I'm accompanied by my Number Two: A, a young and outstanding pilot who's always in the right place. The two of us climb and manoeuvre in formation as if at an air show.

I call target identification, A confirms that he's identified it too, and the climb turns into a steep dive towards the ground. Between identification and aiming there's a little time to look to the sides, to pick out other missiles in the air, and even to steal a glance at the other pilots in the formation. From the radio traffic I learn that R and Guri are still flying.

Another few seconds and we're diving towards the ground. Around us are mushrooms of fire and smoke, evidence of missiles heading for us from the Egyptian

144

battery. Speed, lost during the climb, now gathers anew and if we don't reduce power we'll pass the limits.

I have to bring the nose around to target and, while diving, take aim. The sights are sensitive to any movement and we aim straight at the centre of an SA-3 battery. A squeeze on the trigger. The aircraft shudders and, according to pre-arranged sequence, all the bombs are released, one after the other, with a split second between them. We're free from a multi-ton load and the aircraft at once becomes light and quick. If we haven't been hit by now, no one will get us. Immediately we manoeuvre right and left in a dive. The airplane seems happy to display its true form, moving with utmost ease, having been released from the cumbersome load.

There's smoke mushrooming everywhere; everyone has attacked his target. And here's another call. 'I'm hit!' This time it's Doron Shalev. Rotten luck – after the bomb release.

Following my pull-out I establish contact with all the pilots, receive a report of the hits on target and am free to deal with the crippled aircraft. Guri has been able to pull up a bit, but is forced to bail out and hide in the marshes on the banks of the Canal. Shalev bails out past the Canal in the area between our forces and the enemy lines. Amnon sees him eject and remains behind to circle overhead. We report the bail-out and direct the rescue forces, but the Egyptians race in first. The only one able to fly on is R; he turns towards Refidim, with everyone offering help and suggestions. I order everybody else home and stay with R until Refidim. His aircraft has been badly hit; with impressive skill he brings it in for an emergency landing.

We gathered for the debriefing, agitated and hurting. We had left two crews out there: Guri Palter and his navigator, Yitzhak Baram, who would later be killed in an accident; and Doron Shalev, who is also no longer with us, and his navigator, Lev-Ari.

From an operational standpoint the success was complete, the missile complex array was destroyed, and we had freedom of action in the northern front on both sides of the Canal. It also turned out to be the turning point in the struggle between missile and airplane.

We did it!

Chapter 27
SKIES CLEAR OF MIGS

Lieutenant Colonel (Res) G, today an El Al pilot, holds the Israel Air Force (and possibly world) record for aerial jet victories: during his years as a Mirage pilot he downed seventeen enemy aircraft. His story deals with the air battles he fought during the Yom Kippur War, by the end of which he had racked up eleven victories.

Somehow there was a special chemistry between me and Refidim, the air base in the Sinai. I was one of the first to land there during the Six Day War and the first to do intercept duty there. After the war, ten of my victories were through Refidim. It's too bad there's no way to convey the special feeling Refidim gave the Air Force squadrons. There was an air of absolute freedom, a kind of Wild West feeling; in fact, 'Texas' was Refidim's nickname, especially because of these wild scrambles which led to the free-for-all, 'reach-for-it' dogfights. If there were such a thing as an aerial Western, Refidim would be the local classic.

I began the Yom Kippur War on my home court, Refidim. I was sent there for the usual Friday–Saturday alert and couldn't have imagined that that weekend would become a milestone in the history of Israel. The circle I made in my calendar around 6 October 1973 was only to remind myself that I had alert duty on that date.

I went down to Refidim on the Friday morning with no special intuitive feeling. That afternoon the base commander showed up at the intercept stand, and said there was word that war was going to break out, we should be prepared. I was the senior rank at the intercept stand. I gathered all the mechanics, we distributed personal weapons and showed everyone how to behave under fire and what they had to do. But aside from this there was no special plan.

In the evening we saw a film and went to bed. On Saturday morning they called me from headquarters and told me to return there because war appeared certain; at the time I held a post on the General Staff. They sent a replacement and by 9:30 I was on my way. I had a strange feeling as I travelled from Dov field to headquarters. Tel Aviv was silent; ours was just about the only vehicle on the street. (Yom Kippur is the holiest Jewish day, and in Israel everything literally closes down, including traffic.) So the Yom Kippur War didn't catch me at the hottest spot, but rather at the safest location. I spent most of it at HQ. On the days I was able to get to my squadron, I did nothing special, save for patrols. I had a feeling the war was going to go by and that I would be left out.

On 18 October I was flying out of Refidim. It was towards dusk. They had sent me and my Number Two to 'turn out the lights' over the Canal. I asked Number Two to lead instead, thinking it might be due to my own bad luck that I wasn't meeting up with any MiGs. He refused. They sent us to the area of the pontoon bridge over the Canal, following reports of Egyptian bombing. By then it was quite dark and almost nothing was visible. Suddenly we saw the flash of napalm and I noticed a Mi-8 helicopter rolling barrels of the material on our boys. I went over and blasted the helicopter with my guns and it literally splattered on the waterline. We continued to Refidim and went over to alert.

I was given a Mirage which, that afternoon, had passed through the explosion of a MiG-17 it had helped shoot down. The Mirage had come through in one piece, but was completely blackened; when I came over the mechanics were still hard at work scraping off the soot. There was already a feeling that this was the end and I thought I was going to finish the war with just the helicopter. I was wrong.

The next afternoon we were scrambled to the north of the Bitter Lake. The Egyptians had a special method of attacking: they would come in low with great waves of aircraft, pull up while turning, hit parallel to the Canal and immediately break back to their territory. We thus had very little time to catch them.

We arrived over the Israeli bridgehead and discovered four or five pairs of Su-7s turning left to go in on our troops. We went in after them. I fired a missile at the last aircraft, which exploded right away. Their lead pair managed to drop their bombs on the 'compound' where our forces gathered prior to crossing. Their leader turned to get away, with me right after him. I chased him at low level, which, along with the high speed, caused the aircraft to shake; this in turn made it difficult to get my sights on him until just before the wall of Egyptian anti-aircraft fire, when I managed to hit him with a burst and shoot him down.

We returned home feeling pretty good. But the day was not yet over. At around 4:30 they scrambled us once more to the same area, where the Egyptians were again trying the same tactic. Again I came back with two victories, this time Su-20s. This battle included a little story which no one's forgotten to this day. Aside from the Mirages which participated on our side there were also Phantoms. A quartet slipped in behind the first wave of Egyptian attackers so that the Phantoms were sandwiched in front of the second wave. The bomb run didn't come off this time, but one of the Sukhois got in behind a Phantom and really put him on the spot. My partner closed in on the Sukhoi, but we feared the Egyptian would manage to shoot down the Phantom before we got him. I didn't know the Phantom's call sign and couldn't warn its pilot. When I realized the situation was getting bad I called over the radio, 'Phantoms, break!' My partner managed to down the Sukhoi, but afterwards they began to say in the Air Force that when I arrived at a battle, I would call for everyone to break, so they'd leave their MiGs all to me.

I returned to Refidim. The base was in pretty high spirits, with eleven enemy aircraft shot down. A large part of the war's air battle was waged from this base and the IDF right now was winning. That night there was a big party with lots of performers who came down from the north.

The next morning, the 20th, I was scrambled a number of times, but there was no contact. At around 4:30 we were scrambled again, towards Jebel Ubayid. We were by now used to the Egyptians coming at this hour and quickly found a pair of MiG-21s at 10,000 feet, pulling north in a left-hand turn. We released our drop tanks and raced after them. I reached a good position behind the second one and, at a range of about 1000 metres, launched a Shafrir missile and blasted him. I was still involved in the launch when we suddenly saw ten pairs of MiG-21s mushrooming at us from below, as if they had set a trap, had caught us and were heading up towards us with a highly advantageous number.

We split into two pairs and began fighting. It turned into chaos. My partner went at one of the MiGs, launched a missile which seemed to hit, but he left the fight and went home. The other two Mirages were also headed for home, though not before one of them had shot down another MiG. During all this time I was chasing my own MiG. He was doing all sorts of crazy manoeuvres at low altitude, kicking up dust from the ground every time he came out of his dive. I was behind him doing the same things. In the meantime a number of MiGs tried to get in behind me; it was clear that if I couldn't get my sights on the MiG in front, no one would be able to get theirs on me. In the end, with some kind of a pulling tactic, I managed to get in a burst and shoot down the MiG. At this point the rest of the aircraft from my formation were gone and I was all alone with about ten MiGs.

As soon as I finished with my MiG, I broke and saw that the two MiGs to the rear had launched missiles. These missed and passed by. I wanted to turn after the MiGs, but at that moment I saw flashes out ahead; two other MiGs had launched missiles at me from in front. I hunched down in my seat and tensed up until the missiles passed. Immediately there was another pair of MiGs behind and I had to break. In reality their superiority in numbers was no great problem, because only two or three could be in my rear at a time. There's simply no more room. The real problem was that, because of their great numbers, I didn't have a moment to catch my breath, get set up, or initiate my own offensive action.

Once, when I broke away from a pair of MiGs to my rear, they passed by and climbed. I was able to raise my nose, get off a burst and shoot one down before having to break again. And this went on – breaks and letups and breaks and all – at extremely low altitude.

The fight went on this way for a few minutes, with me breaking and manoeuvring like crazy. Meanwhile, some of the MiGs broke off, leaving only a quartet. I threw two of them forward and right afterwards broke from the second pair, which were also flung ahead. I looked back and saw no more MiGs behind.

The second pair pulled up hard and went over on their backs, as if to do a loop. I went vertical and caught one of them inverted, with me coming in on the perpendicular. I fired a long burst at the cockpit area; the MiG did not catch fire, but it completed its loop – and continued straight into the ground, with almost no explosion. This was my fourth MiG of the dogfight.

I broke right away to frustrate any attack from the rear, but there was no one there. Suddenly the skies were completely clear of MiGs, a truly surprising contrast after all the pressure and gs and enemy planes.

Back at Refidim, the mechanics were waiting to pull me from the aircraft. I simply didn't have the strength to get out by myself.

On the last day of the war, 24 October, I was sent with another three aircraft on an afternoon patrol around the Canal. Over the radio I heard the controller instructing another quartet to engage in air combat. I was told to keep patrolling. I ignored this and went looking for the fight. I discovered a pair of Mirages flying west to east; for a second I thought these were Libyans, but became convinced they were ours, returning home, low on fuel.

In the distance I saw three explosions; clearly there was a fight and aircraft were getting shot down. I raced in and noticed a pair of aircraft above me flying from south to north. I pulled in after them. I launched a missile in a dive; it struck, but the aircraft did not explode. Just a heavy fuel leak. Too bad, I thought, I'll have to move in to gun range and waste a lot of time. Right then the pilot jumped. I thanked him and went after another pair I had discovered and fired a missile at the one to the rear; it hit and the aircraft exploded. I suffered a compressor stall when the missile passed in front of my nose, but throttled back and recovered.

I went on and discovered another MiG with a Mirage sitting behind it and firing. The MiG didn't appear to be hit, but the Mirage broke off. Over the radio I asked the pilot why he hadn't shot down the MiG and he replied that the Egyptian had already bailed out. It seemed strange, so I went up to the MiG in close formation; indeed, there was an empty cockpit with no pilot, the MiG continuing to fly.

I pulled away and discovered another MiG, gave chase, made it to gun range and blasted him. Now the skies were really free of MiGs.

I returned home. I wasn't drunk with victory; the more planes you shoot down the less excited you get. You do without the ceremonies. You don't even do the traditional victory roll over the base. Of all things, your thoughts centre on the aircraft you didn't shoot down.

Chapter 28
ONE-HANDED AND WITHOUT A BURNER

At the end of the Yom Kippur War, Brigadier General B was decorated with Israel's third highest award for valour for his 'performance throughout the war', according to the citation. The following chapter describes some of the episodes which won him the medal.

On the second day of the Yom Kippur War I was hurt in a flying accident and sent to the hospital. I returned, grounded, to the squadron; I couldn't use my right hand. A week later squadron leader Avi Lanir was killed in action and, as his deputy, I was given command.

I felt extremely uncomfortable sending my men into battle while I stayed behind, so somehow I managed to barge my way into the air and returned to operational status as a pilot from the ranks. Actually, my fingers wouldn't function individually; this affected all the actions in the plane that required a gentle touch of the hand. As it happened, it didn't adversely affect my performance; on one of my first flights I managed to shoot down a Syrian MiG one-handed. A few days later I took part in a large dogfight that later became known as the last battle of the Yom Kippur War.

I was leading a four-plane flight of Mirages on a patrol to protect other aircraft that were on an attack mission east of Suez City. We were warned that enemy planes were about to show, and that a dogfight with our strike aircraft was a possibility. On the way there I suffered a malfunction that

152

forced me to turn off the afterburner and fly on a 'dry' engine. In this type of situation one should leave everything and go home – these are not the right conditions for getting into a dogfight. But since I had just returned to flying I couldn't allow myself to exit the war without contributing my share. Thus, rather than setting the proper example, I stayed with the formation and went into the battle.

We arrived on the scene to see four MiGs moving in on our attacking aircraft. We pulled towards them and split up the formation, each of us taking a MiG. Suddenly, four more MiGs came in and pulled for a fight. We then heard over the radio that more of our aircraft were joining in. A real party was shaping up.

I set myself up on one of the MiGs and fired a missile; he managed to break and caused it to miss. I got set up on him from a new position, with Number Four latching on as well. I fired a second missile and at the same time noticed Number Four's, which was a few seconds ahead of mine. But I saw my missile race through the air, manoeuvre and hit – and the MiG went up in flames. (Neither Four nor I received credit for this MiG, which was divided among other pilots.)

I relit the afterburner because my speed was far too low for this battle, but I soon realized that I had to shut down, because it was too dangerous. From that moment on I flew without an afterburner; this kept me from initiating attacks against aircraft at my altitude and speed, so I now looked for those flying below me, hoping I could use my height advantage as a substitute for the burner.

I spotted a plane 5000 feet below and knew I had only one chance to make it straight into gun range. I got in very close, about 200 metres. Since I couldn't set my sights perfectly I fired instinctively – and a very convincing burst of shells set the MiG burning like a torch.

I hadn't even managed a sigh of relief when I noticed a MiG approaching my Number Three. Since he was above me, I tried to raise my nose with what speed I had and fire long-range bursts, hoping to convince him to leave Number Three alone. The MiG pilot was not convinced, but Number Three now noticed him and performed a manoeuvre that brought the MiG out front.

I had to regain lost time because I now saw another MiG flying below. I dropped down on him in almost the same way

153

I had with the other. This time I couldn't get close, so I came in at the maximum range that would still allow me to bring him down. I set up my sights nicely, pressed the trigger and a short burst was enough to set the MiG on fire.

I was in a MiG victory trance. My mind went blank. I looked for another MiG even lower, flew around and found one 1000 feet beneath me. I dropped down, got set up well and launched. The missile hit. There was a puff of smoke, but it was not enough to bring him down. I couldn't continue the pursuit because I was too low and short on fuel. It was just the right time to go home.

As I banked I spotted another MiG out of the corner of my eye. I couldn't resist the urge and zeroed in. I checked my ammo gauge: I had three more shells on the left side and two on the right – enough to shoot down a MiG. I pressed the trigger and got off a single burst. Pop – and that was it. The shells hit but the MiG kept on flying. Now, short of fuel and without ammunition, it really was time to get home and keep myself out of trouble.

I dropped down low in a descending turn; but the MiG I had just hit now banked towards me and started giving chase. This wasn't good; I had no ordnance on the wings and no afterburner and couldn't get into a scrap. What should I do? I tried sticking as close to the ground as I could and waited for the MiG to come into range. He came in to 1500 metres and then closed in even more. I waited for him to launch a missile – which was all I could do. At about 1000 metres I saw the missile being launched, broke hard and managed to evade it.

The MiG got up and out, and above him I saw one of our Mirages giving chase. I asked the Mirage pilot to shoot the MiG down, but the MiG then came in for another pass – this time from 900 metres. It didn't launch a missile because it was apparently out; I assumed the pilot would now try to shoot me down with gunfire. I waited for him to come closer and closer, into gun range. Cannons aren't like missiles – shells fly very fast, and a gun fired under good conditions hits home.

At a shorter range – the closest I would allow anyone to get behind me – I broke very hard. At that moment I saw sparks coming from under the MiG's belly; I realized the Mirage was firing at it. The MiG didn't go down – it pulled up and over me.

I shouted to the Mirage, 'Well, are you going to shoot him down or not?' This apparently did the trick; the Mirage pilot finally brought him down.

That was it. I was able to catch my breath, cross the Canal at low altitude and pull home for a landing.

Chapter 29
RESCUE FROM THE HERMON SUMMIT

Sometime after the end of the Yom Kippur War, an infantry force was trapped on the summit of Mount Hermon. All attempts at rescue failed, and there was concern for the lives of the trapped soldiers. Two Sea Stallion helicopters were sent on a rescue mission in severe winter weather. The first to land on the mountain top was piloted by Colonel S; right after him came the second helicopter, flown by Major D.

I've already rescued enough people to relate to each rescue as something special. But this one was really unusual. From the start, we knew about the drama up there on the heights of the Hermon. We knew that helicopters from another squadron had tried to rescue the trapped men, but hadn't succeeded. We knew an infantry unit had tried to reach them and in turn had had to be rescued. We knew a horrible storm was raging on the Hermon summit and that visibility was from three to ten metres. We knew we could be hit without warning by a Syrian missile. We knew all these things. But we also knew we were the last chance the trapped men had of getting out alive.

In November 1973, an infantry force was sent to the top of Mount Hermon to hold the summit – 6800 feet above sea level – and to establish an observation post. Haste was vital, so the force challenged the mountain without equipment or preparation for the weather up top. The soldiers spread out on three hilltops along the summit. Only with great difficulty were they able to dig foxholes in the rocky ground. The supplies flown up to them weren't suitable for the terrain; tents for protection against the prevailing cold didn't arrive; matches were scarce; there was a shortage of personal equipment. The only consolation, if you could call it that, was a large shipment of cigarettes – enough, according to one of the men, to kill the whole Syrian army with cancer.

There were Syrian commando squads near the summit, 600 or 700 metres from the force. Every night, to keep the Syrians at a distance, the soldiers rolled grenades down the slopes of the mountain. There was only one exchange of fire between the Israeli force and the Syrian commandos; following this the Syrians withdrew from around the Israeli emplacement.

At first the weather was okay. The men could see the Syrian Army movements, Syrian villages on the slopes, and deep into Lebanon. On clear days the visibility extended to Damascus and they could even identify the city's airfield.

And then the storm broke out. One evening the skies darkened and all hell was let loose. The wind brought with it a terrible cold. After a day or two the cold turned to sleet and the sleet to snow; everything froze: first the food, then the water, then the gas and finally the men themselves. They had no real protection against the cold; they were spread out on the hillocks, completely exposed in trenches or shallow foxholes.

The only barrier between the men and the storm was crude improvisation. Many retreated into feelings of hopelessness and became apathetic to their surroundings. A few sat in their foxholes all the time without eating, drinking, or doing a thing.

On the third night of the storm a tremendous bang shook the position. Though the men at first thought it was a Syrian attack, they did nothing. 'Our tent was so tiny and surrounded by such a fog,' one of them said later, 'that I hoped the Syrians simply wouldn't find us.' Later it turned out that lightning had struck the outpost's phone line, and telephone communications were cut off. The only contact with the rear was now a wireless set, which relayed instructions to try and make it out on foot.

Preparations took about an hour at the height of the

storm, when the snow was lashing at the men without letup. It was impossible to open one's eyes. One of the soldiers blacked out before he even started to move.

The column headed out through the snow. Bent under the fury of the wind and worn down by exhaustion and cold in a scene reminiscent of the World War Two battle for Stalingrad, they pulled themselves through the storm. One after the other they began to shed equipment, throwing away even their sleeping bags, without which it would be impossible to stay alive.

After two hours it was apparent they were going in circles; they decided to give up and go back to the outpost. Luckily, the snow had not yet covered their tracks, and the equipment they had discarded served as markers. Totally exhausted, they reached the emplacement and radioed their failure to break out. A short while later they received word that a ground force was setting out to rescue them; they waited in vain for the force's arrival; in the morning they received the bitter message that the rescue force had got stuck, one of their number had frozen to death and others had returned completely exhausted to their base. To make the bleak picture complete the men were informed that the Air Force would not be able to come to their aid in such weather. No helicopter, so they were told, could land on the mountain in these conditions.

The soldiers were beyond despair. Alone they couldn't make it out; a ground force had failed to rescue them, and at a high price; the Air Force couldn't land on the mountain. No options were left. They reconciled themselves to the fact that they wouldn't get out alive, and waited for death.

The Air Force continued to look for a way to get the trapped men off the summit. My helicopter took off from Mahanayim loaded with crates of winter supplies, including snowshoes. We flew north over the Hula Valley, the whole time hearing over the radio the met. reports and the call sign of the trapped force. Winds on the mountain were gusting at fifty to sixty knots and temperatures were below zero. We were worried about visibility, which was from three to ten metres. A few times we heard joyous shouts over the radio that the visibility was now fifty metres, but even with this we couldn't do much.

The problem was how to get to the mountain through the

clouds. At some point someone came up with the idea of sending a Phantom to fly above Lebanon to look for holes in the clouds. When a hole was found we would try to slip through it to the summit.

We waited around Kibbutz Snir, on the foothills of the Hermon. The Phantom pilot reported an opening in the cloud that was crossing the Lebanese coast eastward. We took off, rose above the cloud and decided to fly over the opening. The clouds were very thick. We moved with the opening eastward towards the peak of Hermon, easy to pick out, flashing in its whiteness, for the snow was lying only on the mountain top.

I descended through the hole towards the white of the snow and flew very close to ground level, knowing I had to come in from the east to get on to the summit. Another cloud suddenly covered the hole. Luckily I was familiar with the summit from previous landings.

I hung inside the cloud and flew towards a black spot, which turned out to be a depot for jerrycans near the planned landing site. If I hadn't been familiar with the area, I would have thought I had missed the objective and wouldn't have landed.

We put down in the darkness and right away half-frozen soldiers materialized from every direction, some carried in sleeping bags and hooked up to infusions. The weakest were loaded on to the helicopter. The rest waited for the second Sea Stallion.

The second Sea Stallion, piloted by Major D, followed the first into the mountain clouds.

I knew about the condition of the trapped force. Of course I didn't feel the cold, the loneliness or the despair, but I knew our squadron had landed them on the Hermon – and I knew we had to get them out.

A heavy cloud wrapped the Hermon and it was clear we wouldn't make it straight to the top from down below. I couldn't see the summit at all because the cloud was sitting hard on it. I flew east and descended towards Syria, where the cloud was quite thin. I dropped down, not aware of a strong wind, because as long as you're not in it you don't know its strength. Helicopter pilots have a concept known as

159

'descending wind': if you get into one you won't always be able to get out. When I closed in on the mountain I immediately went into this descending wind; the Sea Stallion began to lose altitude and drop down the ridge towards Syria – in daylight, with all of Syria waiting and watching. My co-pilot was silent as we backed away a little from the mountain and started to climb, waiting to see where the missile would come from.

The wind was strong and we didn't know exactly where we were. After a few minutes of flight the clouds thinned out and we began to see ground. We came out a little to the north, and dropped down inside a hole in the cloud. Where were we? I didn't know. We saw a tree-covered area, pretty hillocks, but nothing familiar. At this point I cut myself off from the controller and improvised as best I could.

We began to fly south. Where were we going? Where were we? We didn't know. Suddenly a flash of inspiration: hold on, the summit of the Hermon is the highest part – so I'll ascend close to ground level. And this is what I did. The terrain began to rise steeply and we knew we were approaching the summit. We flew very slowly, and suddenly saw ice and snow instead of trees and hillocks. Then something weird – all sorts of spools. Afterwards I learned it was frozen concertina wire. The fog was very thick; I decided to land right away and go on when the fog passed. Touching down at the first spot I could, I looked to my left and saw a surrealistic picture: standing there in the fog was a group of people and in the background a smoke grenade. We opened the door and turned on the heater full blast. The people charged in and ran to hug us joyously. We took off and flew south, to another world.

As a Sea Stallion pilot I am usually unable to talk with people flying in the back. I generally see eyes back there, looking at me in worry or amazement. After this flight I began to look on soldiers a little differently. Before, they had only been numbers: twenty-five, thirty-five soldiers. Quantities. I had related to them only in terms of payload and the difficulty of taking off and landing. No more. This flight shocked me. When I saw those people standing in the snow, in total despair and frozen stiff, I said to myself: 'Where were you? Drinking coffee, getting into your helicopter, coming back to your coffee. And they ... only God knew what these soldiers had been through.'

160

Chapter 30
TO ENTEBBE AND BACK

The famous rescue flight is described by Brigadier General V, commander of the Hercules squadron.

On 27 June 1976, at 6:45 in the morning, Singapore Airways flight 763 landed at Athens airport from Bahrain. Four of the five disembarking passengers, a woman and three men, made for the departure hall, to wait patiently for their next flight: Air France 139 to Paris.

At 11:30 the Air France Airbus made a smooth landing on the Athens runway, and thirty-six passengers got off. Fifty-eight others, among them the quartet from Bahrain, headed towards the Airbus waiting on the tarmac.

No one was on duty at the metal detector through which the travellers passed, and the policeman at the x-ray machine paid little heed to the picture on the monitor's screen. The four made their way unhindered on to the Airbus.

At 12:30 the aircraft's wheels left the ground and the pilot, Captain Michel Bak, climbed steadily towards 31,000 feet. The cabin crew started to prepare lunch for the 246 passengers.

Just eight minutes after take-off the hijackers made their move. The woman left her seat in first class and took up position at the front of the passenger compartment. Two of the men stood up holding pistols and threatened the passengers in tourist class. The third man, pistol in one hand and a grenade in the other, broke into the cockpit. Air France 139 had been hijacked.

The first thought to go through my mind when I heard of the hijacking was, What does this have to do with us? The aircraft was French, and the French government would have to grapple with the problem. But later, when it turned out that dozens of Israelis were aboard the aircraft, which had meanwhile landed in Benghazi, Libya, I understood the problem was no longer French, but ours.

When it was learned later that day that the aircraft had gone deeper into Africa, to Entebbe in Uganda, the problem took on serious dimensions. Right away we began to plough through contingency plans. From the first it was clear that the only way for us to get to Entebbe was in the Hercules. Range was no problem, as IAF C130s had flown regularly to Uganda until Idi Amin had broken diplomatic relations with Israel in March 1972.

Operational planning went into high gear, and on Tuesday we were ready with a detailed layout. But by that night, knowing that the hijackers had separated the Jewish passengers, 105 in number, from the non-Jews, and released the latter, the plan was no longer viable.

The phone caught me in the middle of a wedding in Haifa. I returned right away to Air Force headquarters and we, the Hercules crews, along with army officers, began to work like crazy. Together we came up with a new plan that took into account a night landing on an unlit runway. The Chief of Staff demanded a demonstration to prove it could work. The demonstration was set for Friday 2 July, at Ophir base in Sharm e-Sheikh; in certain ways conditions there resembled those at Entebbe. On Friday morning I undertook a preliminary flight above the Ophir runway for practice. I wanted the presentation to work.

That evening the CoS, Motta Gur, and Air Force chief Benny Peled boarded the aircraft. We took off from Lod and flew to Ophir. We made two passes, two perfect landings. The CoS slapped me on the shoulder and said, 'I think you'll make it.'

We returned home and took off for another air base to take part in a rehearsal of the ground part of the operation for the Defence Minister, CoS and other officers. The presentation was so successful that the observers did not even see the aircraft. This, of course, was exactly our aim.

Saturday, 3 July 1976. All the troops, including air crews, gathered for a final briefing. Every participant fully understood his role, but the green light hadn't yet been given for the operation. After the briefing we flew to Ophir, our southernmost airfield, to refuel. The assault force, along with a black Mercedes and two Landrovers, were in the lead aircraft. The second and third aircraft carried guard and back-up forces. The fourth aircraft was empty, reserved for the hostages.

My aircraft was loaded beyond allowable limits, even according to the standards of war. I wasn't sure that anyone in Israel or elsewhere had ever tried to take off in these conditions. The outside temperature was 39° centigrade; this kind of heat dramatically lowers an airplane's performance capabilities.

I ran the aircraft down the runway but the air speed indicator did not rise above eighty to ninety knots, and to leave the ground you need 130. The runway was long, but it seemed to me it was running out. And we weren't gaining speed. For a moment I thought of aborting the take-off. If the aircraft wouldn't lift off, we were going to end up in the water. But then I thought of what would happen if I did not shut down the throttles, and how I'd look to everyone else for the rest of my life. This was the most powerful stimulus to continue the take-off despite everything.

In the end, the aircraft left the runway with great difficulty, its nose heading north. After take-off we turned south; due to the low speed and sluggishness we had to turn in a huge radius, part of it over Saudi Arabia. Only after 100–200 miles did the aircraft really come to life, and we flew uneventfully over the Red Sea towards Uganda.

In mid-flight, after a good number of hours, I considered lying down for thirty minutes or so on the bed installed in the Hercules' cockpit. I thought I'd close my eyes and try to unwind a bit. I looked over at the bed and saw Yoni, the commander of the assault force, lying on it. We usually reserve the bed for the aircrew, but I decided to let him be. I nudged him a bit and stretched out beside him. He was sleeping like a baby. I thought to myself that he would shortly be going into the fire, and here he was sleeping as though he didn't have a worry in the world. I was tremendously impressed.

As we crossed the African coast the weather changed, and we found ourselves in the middle of an electrical storm that forced us to detour dozens of miles. We finally made Lake

Victoria, where my aircraft broke away from the rest to allow me to land first. Hovering at this spot was a typical African cumulo-nimbus about 550 feet from the ground. I couldn't avoid going through it because we wanted precise navigation. As a result we suffered severe turbulence, hail and rain. Static electricity exploded above the aircraft windows in frightful colours.

The runway was fully illuminated; the landing was perfect – no one saw the aircraft. After landing, we taxied to a spot where we planned to offload the troops. The Mercedes and two Landrovers, with Yoni's force inside, left the aircraft right away, passed underneath a wing, and careened off at great speed towards Old Terminal. We continued taxiing and parked the aircraft on the tarmac of New Terminal, where more troops disembarked, these having the double role of guarding the aircraft and taking over New Terminal.

The second Hercules landed while the runway was still fully illuminated. Then the firing began, and all the field lights went out. The third aircraft was in mid-landing when this happened, but it still came down safely. The fourth Hercules was brought down with the aid of emergency lights prepared in advance.

We secured the aircraft for parking and were free to watch what was happening on the field. It was an exhilarating experience seeing the variety of tracers crossing the sky and the giant fire caused when our forces blew up the Ugandan MiGs. We were in continuous contact with the assault force, and knew within minutes that the main part of the operation had been carried out – the terrorists had been killed and the hostages were in our hands. Our joy was watered down by the anguish of hearing of Yoni's death.

We had brought fuel pumps and got organized to refuel on the spot. But then we learned we could land in Kenya to refuel. Because the process of pumping fuel is lengthy and complicated, I decided not to do it, and to keep our time at Entebbe as short as possible to eliminate further danger. The costly pumps ended up remaining behind.

The fourth Hercules, almost totally empty, taxied over to Old Terminal. Soldiers of the assault force were lined up in two rows, leaving a narrow path between them from the terminal door to the lowered ramp of the Hercules. In seven minutes all the hostages, the Air France crew, the dead and wounded were aboard.

164

Forty-five minutes after landing the aircraft took off and was on its way. This moment, when I saw the Hercules with the hostages lift off in the darkness, was one of the highpoints of the mission. All of us were quite moved. With the boys who fought there it would have been possible to hold the field for even two weeks with no serious problem. But the hostages were out.

The other three aircraft, including mine, gathered the troops on the field, while each commander counted his men. The plan for take-off was simple – whoever was ready, left. My aircraft was second; the space between take-offs was just minutes. We headed towards refuelling in Nairobi, set down on the field, and were flooded with questions from the controllers. 'Where are you coming from? What's your nationality? Where are you bound?' Each pilot either came up with some cover story or simply ignored the questions.

The first thing I did on landing at Nairobi was go over to the aircraft with the hostages. I wanted to see them, and it was amazing. Their faces reflected joy, stupefaction, terror – every kind of emotion there is. I tried to question some of them, but wasn't able.

We took off from Nairobi and, starting at three in the morning, while still on our way home, heard news of the operation over Israel Army Radio; you could tell from the announcer's voice that he had his doubts. But afterwards came the official confirmation, and mass hysteria broke out everywhere. I began to understand the meaning the operation had for the country.

After eight uneventful flight hours we landed in Israel. The reception would be difficult to forget; they fell on us and smothered us with hugs and kisses. At that moment I realized I hadn't slept in four days, and the only thing that interested me was resting my head on a pillow and sleeping for at least forty-eight hours straight.

We finally got away from all the hugs, and each of us went home. I hoped at least there I'd be able to rest. But waiting for me were all the kids from the kindergarten holding hundreds of roses. And they wouldn't let me go to sleep. After this little celebration came a gathering of family, friends, and acquaintances. Well, we sat around until the wee hours, and sleep had to wait for some other time, much, much later.

Chapter 31
KEEPING THE PROMISE

On 27 June 1979 the first air combat in history between F-15s and MiG-21s took place over southern Lebanon. The result: five Syrian MiGs downed, and Colonel M kept a promise he had made some time before.

The story of this aerial victory really begins a few years previously, on the day we, the first six pilots sent to learn to fly the F-15, arrived in the US. We showed up for a visit at the McDonnell Douglas factory, where the aircraft are built, in St Louis. We wanted to see 'our' airplanes, the famous first four destined for the IAF. We met the company's test pilots, engineers and managers. We were in the middle of learning about the aircraft and were hungry for every crumb of information on performance and handling. The test pilots seemed the ideal source for this type of information, and we didn't hesitate to pump them dry.

At lunch with the company president, we exchanged compliments. They envied us our operational flights, and we expressed wonder at their being able to fly the world's most advanced aircraft. The conversation rolled on, and I couldn't hold back; I bet everyone there that I would be the first pilot in the world to shoot down a plane with the F-15. Only after the words were out did I realize what I had said. I wasn't even the senior pilot in our group; I was with veteran flyers, real lions, and in front of them I had made this pledge.

But if I said it, I said it. And if you say something you've got to do it, so from that moment on I dreamt of the time I'd get to keep the promise.

After the course was over we returned to Israel and took delivery of the first aircraft. For a year and a half we flew only training flights. Not that we didn't want to fly operational flights. There just weren't any.

During the Litani Operation, in March 1978, we finally flew our first operationl sorties, but there was no contact with the Syrian Air Force, mostly patrols. After Litani, I went to Air Force Flight Academy as commander of the fighter course, and the promise I had made at McDonnell Douglas seemed very distant. Then one day I got a call from B, my squadron leader, who said, 'There's an interesting flight. Want to come?' Of course I did.

When I got to the squadron, it turned out B had put together a formation made up of the first group of F-15 pilots, and we left for a patrol over Lebanon. We patrolled for an hour, and nothing happened. The MiGs never came. We returned, quite disappointed, to the squadron.

We lost out on a 'click'. A click, for those who don't know, is connected to the squadron's duty rotation. A pilot who goes out on an operational sortie has passed a click, and now it's someone else's turn to fly. Until you get another turn – until the next click – you have to wait a bit. I trusted that B wouldn't let me wait too long.

Towards the end of June 1979 things were heating up along the Syrian border. A number of times they tried to interfere with our aircraft, and I could smell my chance coming around again.

On 27 June, at ten in the morning, right in the middle of a meeting with the head of the Flight Academy, a phone call. B was on the line. I guessed what he wanted. 'Be here within twenty minutes,' he said. I am a disciplined soldier. Within twenty minutes I was at the squadron, and wasn't surprised to find once more the others from the first F-15 group. 'This is the day,' said B with absolute certainty, and we got into our aircraft, hoping that this time he was right.

We are flying to Lebanon to patrol not far from Sidon, standing guard over aircraft of ours on a strike. We don't even get in two legs – and here are the blips of MiGs on our radar scopes, come to break up the raid. And then over the radio we receive instructions to turn back towards the sea.

We're sure that for all sorts of reasons, they've decided to avoid confrontation. I feel a tremendous disappointment.

But a few minutes later we get the much-hoped-for green light; before the controller can even finish his message my drop tanks are already released and on their way down. Together with B I make a nice bank back into Lebanon and dash off towards the Syrians.

We have a wonderful system in our hands, and right away we know we have excellent launch conditions. I ask B, who is leading, for permission to open fire. He doesn't answer, the scoundrel, and I pick up on his trick; he simply wants to launch first. And that's what happens. First he launches, and only afterwards does he give me permission.

It's a very clear day, and the skies are wondrously blue to the east. We're a little high for a dogfight, and I've never before witnessed from this altitude the scene now unfolding before my eyes: Two missiles, mine and B's, etching a burning tail, just like in *Star Wars*, far, far into the blue skies, and I'm expecting a red-orange-black explosion. But a reasonable time for a hit elapses – and no explosion!

There are a lot of aircraft in the sky. Two or three flights of MiGs, us and some Kfirs. In short, real bedlam.

I decide that the surest thing is to revert to old habits. I stick my head out and look around. And indeed, from far off come two MiGs, crossing my flight path, a bit lower. And then, as if someone says to them, 'Watch out: don't maintain that heading because there's danger,' they reverse bank, and in doing so give a silent signal that they've seen us and are reacting.

But an F-15 is an F-15, and it has a few surprises of its own. I press the specific button, and the missile heads straight out. As it departs it strikes the MiG in front, no messing around, and the MiG simply breaks in two. I've never seen such a thing, although this is my seventh aerial victory, and I've also witnessed other pilots' hits.

I'm euphoric. I'm dead sure no other gunfighter has beaten me to the draw; this is the first MiG to fall in this battle, and the first to fall to an F-15. I'm so overjoyed I don't even try to shoot down his partner – a mistake I'll never make again: I teach the young pilots that the battle is never over, even after the downing of an airplane. But this time I can do nothing; the uplifting feeling is stronger than I am.

Very quickly the calls race over the radio. 'Got one.' 'Shot one down.' And I realize the booty from this dogfight won't be small. The whole thing is finished in about a minute; the battle's over and we return home. Everyone reports on what he's done; I wait until they're all through and broadcast the sentence they remember to this day: 'Say what you want, but I was first.'

It's not that I'm so great. It's just a matter of luck – you have to be in the right place at the right time. This fight was not really so tough. It was actually quite easy – the MiG simply got stuck right in front of my face, and that was it. It would be impossible to compare this battle to the practice dogfights we wage at the squadron. They are really the toughest.

Chapter 32
BAGHDAD BOMBING DIARY

Captain R, an F-16 pilot, was one of the aviators chosen to take part in the bombing of the Iraqi nuclear reactor. This chapter is part of a diary he kept during preparations for the mission and includes his personal impressions of the sortie itself.

Friday, 6 May 1981 We already know that the day set for the raid is Sunday. The aircraft to be used for the operation have been carefully chosen. Every operational area on the base has been closed off; we park in a place set aside for us. The ground crews are virtual prisoners out on the field; we're getting things organized at the squadron, with just the squadron leader and base commander out making sure everything is going well. Maybe they know, maybe they don't.

In the evening we have a stormy game of basketball, which another squadron wins, basically due to bad calls, as well as more balls in the hoop. A few songs with the help of a guitar and to bed. Tomorrow will be a long day of studying.

Saturday, 7 May 1981 We go down to the squadron at 9:30 in the morning. The mission leader writes on the board and the briefing begins. We carefully go over every little thing, starting with material for the flight, going out to the aircraft, taxiing and the fuel. We discuss every possibility of winds, malfunctions, message transmissions, silence, take-off, navigation – in short, every minute of the flight is gone over in depth. On the wall is a detailed map. Everyone readies his own flight materials with his particular markings. The briefing is over at 5:00 and we put everything back in the safe; the picture drawn by 'the artist' of how things will look to the pilot in his bombing pass is inside our heads. A guy from Field Security accompanies us with a severe look on his face. Everyone goes to his room; the Old Man stays to study things some more.

In the room, the gallows humour begins; Major 'Lucky' will luck out and make the centre gallows. The Kibbutznik can't fall asleep. The Systems Man thinks about whether to take along some margarine for the long flight. I fall asleep, burdened by a sense of mission mixed with fatalism.

Sunday, 8 May 1981 The minibus picks us up to go to breakfast and to the squadron. We see our twin-tailed, twin-engined brothers on final approach; they land and taxi in. Hugs, kisses and immediately to the briefing. The room is packed: the Chief of Staff, 'Raful' Eitan, who is in mourning for his pilot son; Air Force GOC David Ivri, top army brass and other VIPs who have pushed in.

The mission leader quickly repeats yesterday's performance, using various pyrotechnics. The idea is to impress the commanders so they'll see they're in this together with guys who know what they're doing and will do it well. I don't have to listen, everything's already clear. I'm familiar with every minute of the navigation; every turn, path, stream and waypoint. The acceleration, turning on the radar, the search for MiGs, the rivers, the wall on the horizon, and the Artist's picture are in my head.

'On your shoulders rests the future of the State of Israel,' the CoS cuts into my thoughts. He explains the political and security background, domestic and international, that led to the decision, made a while back.

Handshakes with the Air Force GOC and the CoS. They seem to pause to look each one of us in the eye, as if to say, I hope all of you come back. The experts – the meteorologist, the planner – give us a distant look, as if they don't know us and therefore won't feel bad.

And now for a festive lunch, like the Last Supper. On the way we pass by the bathroom; this is my fourth piss this hour.

Palms sweaty and feeling a little uncomfortable, I hug a friend from the twin-tail squadron. We look each other in the eye – no need to speak.

We go back to the squadron to put on our G-suits, to check once more whether the pistol is loaded. And suddenly the speakers call out: Everyone to the briefing room. There they inform us the show is off, apparently for political reasons. Hey, wait! I've already stopped being afraid. I've already marked everything on the map. I'm already on my way! What an anticlimax. Disappointment. A duel with fate that never took place.

We pack up, get into swimsuits and go to the beach. The Kibbutznik lies on his back and looks up at the sky like he can't believe it.

Wednesday, 3 June 1981 Feverish preparations for a trip. Rounding up command cars, jeeps, jerrycans, food, utensils and everything else. In the afternoon a call from HQ: 'Boys, there's tension. It looks like you won't be taking your trip.'

The next day the picture is clear. The mission's set for Sunday. At least they didn't ruin our weekend, which passes lazily.

Sunday, 7 June 1981 A fast morning briefing and we quickly load our equipment. The same briefing. This is it. Everything moves. A trip to the bathroom, but we don't drink any water; we don't want any pressure on our bladders. And here it is, two o'clock. Time to go. The G-suit zipper heaves slightly – the suit is weighed down by additional equipment: torso, helmet and VTR cassette – and out we go.

I arrive at my aircraft and look it over. 'This is my fourth straight flight with you. Don't cheat me now.' I pat the angle-of-attack instrument and smack one of the bombs. The technical officer comes up to the ladder and looks at me with his cunning eyes. 'Send regards from the boys in Ramat Gan,' he says.

Climb to the cockpit; a thorough going-over of the switches – there's time.

I don't wait forty seconds and already move the throttle to idle. The engine catches; the temperature gauge begins to rise as usual and stabilizes at 550 degrees. I move around in the seat and settle in. 'We'll have a few hours to pass together; you and me, iron and flesh.' I see the Artist running around worried – it seems something's broken down and he's switching aircraft. What's important is that all's well with me. A long zeroing-out process – thirty minutes. No need to rush.

I taxi out slowly. The aircraft is heavy. The sun blazes and I roll over to the fuelling position; I open the fuel cover and wait to see the amount slowly rise. Everyone around me is guzzling fuel, but with me the son of a bitch refuses to rise to the required amount. 'Switch bowser,' I tell the mechanic. It doesn't help. The pressure I'm under! It's already 3:55. Okay, I know the plan; it's set up with a good margin of safety for fuel. I head out.

We straighten out on the runway in formation for take-off, 300 metres from one another. The digital clock ticks away; 'take-off in full dry', just like in the Fouga. We'll wait until eighty knots in order to save fuel and only then afterburner. A kick in the ass and we're running. It's heavy. This is quick – 190 knots and immediately to full dry. Wheels up and we settle into a defensive formation. At first we fly with a wonderful view, just like in all those stories, and afterwards dunes and a parched desert vista. But it's most important to maintain position. The minutes go by slowly. The fuel doesn't even itself out at the desired rate; I transfer some to the back to reduce drag. Maybe this will help.

Before releasing my drop tanks I verify that I've done everything through to the end. Switch hands and, ppfffftt, the two of them fly off; how nice. Another reference point and the terrain changes – Iraqland. An occasional truck crosses the desert; and there's the lake with four islands. The waypoint passes and we start to accelerate. We've passed another line of longitude and start opening up into a line astern.

I look at Number Four; he's fast in place. The Old Man's ahead of me and to the right. Number Two's sticking to the ground; 'Up a bit,' I say to myself. We cross a shoreline, to the right a bus with tourists, colourful taxis on the beach – they're having a good time.

Forty miles to pull up and there are no MiGs on radar. I look at it: 'Please say nothing – let us get closer.' And up ahead, a water snake crawling from left to right; the Euphrates. We were here already 2500 years ago. Buildings, an old airfield and power cables along a highway, everything rushes by at headspinning speed. Ten miles. Ahead of me I

173

see the Artist's tower right in my sights. I'm in place. Everyone else is in place, too. I'm dying to piss. A flash in the air and Number One reports, 'Watch out they're firing ack-ack here.' The tumult is already starting. Flashes fill the sky; shells fly along the route. Another second and here's the Tigris. Full burner, I pull, and here, clear in front of me the wall and within, impossible to get it wrong, the dome, silvery in the evening sun. It's 17:35. Seven gs. I flip the aircraft with a lot of speed and already see the smoke rising up – still no great explosion.

I go over on my back – now it's just me, the airplane and the pipper; they're firing heavily from within the structure and the pipper slowly closes in. Don't goof. A little adjustment – and that's it. Now! Two bombs released. Break hard left and look for missiles in the sky. What's this flying? A missile hits the ground below us; 600 knots, full dry, everyone's okay. We race westward with wild exhilaration and a sense of relief. Another moment and fire from the right. The Artist goes straight into the fire, pulls up and it's all right. Flashes cross from left to right. A little further and we climb and slowly gain altitude. Below, the whiteness of the blinding, setting sun. We get into formation and honk like geese. The leader radios, 'We did it!' and about half an hour later the Air Force GOC comes over the horn: 'Now all you have to do is land. Be careful!' I'm worried about my bladder and he's worried about the landing. To each his own.

Minutes before landing: darkness, navigation lights, a wide circuit. If I go around (I have 800 pounds of fuel) I piss in my G-suit. I can't hold it. We land.

I gather up my equipment, signal the mechanics and meet up with my Number Two. A rugged hug, real joy to see his babyface. Back to the squadron without much small talk. Fly home, a kiss for the wife. She still doesn't know what happened.

Chapter 33
EYE OF THE MISSILE ON THE TAIL
OF THE AIRPLANE

*On the fourth day of the 1983 Peace for Galilee Operation
the Israel Air Force stood its greatest test since the 1973 Yom
Kippur War: the destruction of the Syrian missile batteries in
Lebanon's Beka'a Valley. The Syrians scrambled dozens of
fighters to the scene of the battle and while the attack against
the missiles was underway a large-scale dogfight developed
among dozens of aircraft on both sides. Fourteen out of the
nineteen missile batteries were destroyed, three more were hit
and twenty-nine Syrian aircraft were shot down.*

*Major R, author of this chapter, participated in the anti-
missile operation as an F-16 pilot and accounted for the
downing of a Syrian MiG.*

This sortie began on Wednesday morning, 9 June 1982, but
it was born long before, during the Yom Kippur War, when
the Air Force emerged from a confrontation with surface-to-
air missile complexes, its wings a little bent. Nine years had
gone by since then, nine years of precise preparation for this
day. And there was no doubt this day would arrive.

Our squadron was told to set aside a formation for a strike
against SA-2 batteries. It was clear the brunt of the operation
would be assigned to the Phantom squadrons and we could
only hope that we would be given attack missions, as a
contrast to the intercept patrols we had undertaken since the
war broke out. All of us went into operations to see the
orders for the planned mission and to share in the excitement.

175

I figured my chances for participating in the sortie were high enough, but just to be sure I whispered to the proper person my suggestion as to who should be in the formation and I, of course, was included.

In the meantime I was sent to sit on alert. On the way I ran into the squadron leader; I asked him to assign me to the attack formation. He gave me a long look, promised nothing and ran quickly to the squadron.

There was still time until take-off, although the whole Air Force was busy planning the operation. The central computer systems were being fed data; mechanics were loading bombs on the bellies of the aircraft and hanging missiles on the wings; and the pilots were busy studying approach routes, terrain and anti-aircraft threats. For years we had practised for this day and now we had to memorize the correct flight tactics, plan how to evade the missiles and correctly operate all the systems.

For two hours I sat at the intercept stand, with nothing doing; my relief was scrambled into air after just a few minutes of waiting. On any other day I would have given the nearest wall a kick of frustration, but I wasn't sorry I missed the scramble – I had a feeling I would come out ahead. I hurried over to the squadron to discover that this was indeed the case: a formation from my squadron would be attached to one from a sister squadron and I would lead the whole thing. We were to hit a number of missile batteries. Time over target was scheduled for 15:50 hours.

I was allowed to choose my Number Two. I looked around at everyone gathered in the room and only one person was looking me straight in the eye. The matter was closed. I pointed at him and his name immediately went on the board.

They handed out the assignments and we ran to the overall briefing. All the pilots were sitting there listening to the multi-tiered plan. The map could hardly be deciphered for all the arrows and colours. I knew we had planned the operation and it was clear that not a single thing had been left out.

The general briefing was over and I briefed the men of my own formation. The pilots looked at me with concern and I admitted that I too was afraid – afraid of the unknown. I was reminded of stories from the Yom Kippur War and the War of Attrition, the look of horror on the faces of those who came back without their friends, without having executed missions – and I thought about the tremendous effort of the Air Force.

I pre-flighted the aircraft in detail: bomb fins straight; fuses properly set; enough nitrogen in the missile cooling tanks. Someone noticed my concern and comforted me with warm words. I climbed up to the cockpit and sat myself in the seat. That was it; from this moment on I had to go to work.

The canopy closes. Ignition switch to START and the starter turns the engine. RPMS rise quickly and the generator is on line. I turn on all the systems: enter data into the navigation terminal, load the correct plan into the weapons terminal and go over the rest of the switches. Nothing can be overlooked.

And now I taxi. The aircraft is heavy and rolls slowly to take-off position. There, a row of Phantoms and us, a formation of F-16s, like dwarfs next to the F-4s. The base commander arrives at the take-off position and looks at the row of aircraft anxiously. I'm sure his heart is breaking; after all he's used to sitting in the cockpit for missions like this. I instinctively give him the thumbs-up.

Time for take-off. I straighten out and look over my formation partners. They're also thumbs-up. Engine to full burner and the aircraft begins to lumber down the runway. A light pull on the stick and I'm in the air. Wheels up and I stay at low level. Over Acre we get set up into formation and turn north along the Lebanese coast.

Dozens of aircraft appear on the radar screen – the attack is in full swing. At this point we still have no idea as to results, but to tell the truth we're not interested. All we care about is executing our part of the mission.

The radar looks for interceptors and we glide along at low altitude, hugging the ground. Far off to the south we notice the smoke and fire of war, but we're on a circuitous and concealed route. We turn south according to the map and during the turn ground control calls, 'Watch around you for their aircraft.' Indeed, right after the turn, I see on radar aircraft circling above my target.

The range decreases. About ten miles left, less than a minute to target. What do we do? If we go in for the attack we could get in trouble with the MiGs. But if we engage them we won't attack the target. A dilemma. Have to decide right away. No time for what-ifs. Every second the aircraft covers 300 metres and I have to make the right decision. I shoot another glance at the radar and see that according to the direction of the MiGs' turn they won't see us as we pull for the attack. I press the transmit button: 'Switches to "attack".' Now it's clear to everyone that we're going to ignore the MiGs.

A few seconds and we're over the pull-up point. Full burner, nose up and the aircraft climbs at a steep angle. Eyes go from the mountain, along-the-ground features, and converge on the missile battery. Another few seconds and I roll the aircraft over on its back and bring the sights to the target. I've done this tens, maybe hundreds of times during practice. Now it's different. I bring along the sights and already notice flashes of anti-aircraft fire from the battery and its surroundings. No time to be afraid. The centre of the circle is in the middle of the battery. I press the bomb release button and within eighty thousandths of a second the four tons of explosives leave the aircraft and are on their way down.

And now to get out. A break to the right and after about a second I see the explosion in the centre of the battery. 'Two! With me over to air-air.' We drop down into the wadi we had come in from.

The rest of the planes are about three miles to the north and I see a pair of aircraft, one flying towards us, the second setting up to come in. Over the radio comes a call: 'MiGs, MiGs!'

The eye of the missile is on the tail of the airplane – the tone is in my ear – and I release the missile's seeker. It answers enthusiastically and informs me through the computer that it's locked on to the MiG's engine. The angle is about ninety degrees and the MiG's silvery body symbolizes every fighter pilot's dream. The missile slides off the left wing for its designated meeting. The second missile is already set for back-up. Five seconds pass – they seem an eternity – until the missile explodes with a small plume of smoke. Contact. The MiG simply stands still in the air. Another second and his right wing is suddenly torn from place; the aircraft spins and catches fire. A pull on the stick in order to go over him; I see the pilot jump and his parachute opens.

Now to regroup the formation. Number Two lags behind, partly my fault, partly from the heat of excitement, and in another minute we're all on our way home. Two signals that he's short a missile and gives the thumbs-up. The controller calls us. 'Report your results.' Whoever decided to buy the F-16 had this moment in mind. Small, speedy, highly manoeuvrable and capable of carrying ordnance over long distances without trading off its air-to-air capability. I breathe deep and call over the radio, 'Two MiGs, two hits.'

We land. Our individual joy is part of the overall happiness that envelops the whole Air Force when the results of the operation are verified. The siren then cuts off the gaiety. I run off for a patrol in the north. The war goes on.

Chapter 34
LANDING WITH ONE WING

In the summer of 1983, during a practice flight over the Negev Desert, an F-15 and a Skyhawk collided in mid-air. The Skyhawk immediately blew up, but its pilot got out safely. The force of the collision tore off the F-15's right wing. The pilot, Captain (Res) M, continued to fly and successfully landed the aircraft – with only one wing.

I was leading a flight during air-to-air exercises over the Negev. As part of these exercises we were to stage a dogfight with Skyhawks that were doing ground attack practice in the area. I was patrolling over the Nahal Tzin wadi and heard from ground control that the first Skyhawks were heading our way. I sent S, my Number Two, to catch them on the way. I picked them up on radar and gave chase until the spot where S was. The Skyhawks were flying in two formations; I was chasing the second and S the first. We all pulled at the same time: the four Skyhawks, S and I. I felt very uneasy with all this confusion. Maybe I could have intercepted them on the way up, but I was bothered by the disorder and the close quarters and I got up and out.

Now I saw the whole picture below: the first pair of Skyhawks, S, and the leader of the second pair, who was just then turning in underneath me and coming in for the attack. I was still feeling uncomfortable because I could not see all the aircraft. I lowered my nose and launched a missile at their Number One, who was right then coming in for a pass. His

Number Two was a young pilot who couldn't clearly identify the target. He pulled up beyond the allowable height without knowing I was above. He didn't see me and I didn't see him. We collided. His belly, my wing.

At first I didn't realize we had run into each other. I felt a tremendous jolt and thought I had flown through the exhaust of another aircraft. G, a navigator in the squadron flying with me during these exercises, said right away, 'We've hit someone.' Before I could say anything the fireball that had been the Skyhawk passed in front of my eyes. Immediately the radio was full of all kinds of calls about 'someone who had ejected'. I realized the Skyhawk had exploded from the collision and its pilot had automatically been ejected.

A tremendous spume of fuel was coming from my wing and I knew this meant I had been hit seriously. But I didn't yet realize there was no wing at all; I only saw creases, distortions and pieces of metal: the fuel spray hid the place where the wing should have been.

The aircraft went out of control. Though I had the controls full over, I couldn't get the airplane out of its bank or horizontal. It moved in a strange kind of spiral, completely uncontrollable. I told G, 'We're going to bail out. Get ready.' But I was still in no rush to eject, though the greatest fear in bailing out is doing it too late. In addition, the longer you wait, the more speed builds up, and it's undesirable to jump at high speed. But the collision had brought us down to 280–300 knots, so I decided to wait until 6000 feet and then jump.

The whole time I could hear the tumult over the radio about the Skyhawk pilot having bailed out. 'He's ejecting; he's got a chute; he's here; he's there.' At some point I simply turned off the radio and concentrated on my own problem.

None of the cockpit instruments had been affected. Despite this I couldn't hold on to the aircraft. I pulled my head inside the cockpit and saw the electrical control system had disengaged. The F-15 has two control systems, hydraulic and electric. Together they provide an extra few degrees of steering. I quickly re-engaged the electrical system; my right leg was fully extended, ailerons completely to the right and stick almost all the way back. I was slowly able to gain control and bring the aircraft back to the straight and level.

The fear of having to eject didn't let up for a single moment; right after the collision it was clear that sooner or later I'd have to. But now it seemed that I had somehow regained control of the aircraft, I said to myself, 'Hold on, we're not bailing out yet.' Once I had re-engaged the controls the situation looked good; not a single warning light was on; all the hydraulic systems were sealed tight; the other systems were working as if nothing had happened; the navigational computer was working normally. The only thing missing was a warning light to tell me I had no wing . . .

I programmed the co-ordinates of the nearest base into the computer and saw that it wasn't far away. About twenty miles. We turned in that direction and headed there very, very slowly. (I didn't want to turn on the afterburner because I feared this would ignite the fuel streaming from the wing.) We climbed slowly to altitude and brought the aircraft towards the field. I asked my Number Two to come and look me over. He had already passed above us but was sure we had bailed out; he saw an aircraft in the sky with one wing and was sure it couldn't continue to fly. (At this point I still wasn't aware I had no wing.) Number Two checked the aircraft over and said, 'There's very serious damage to your right wing.'

It seemed I had no choice. I would have to bail out. The wing is a fuel tank and the aircraft was seriously low on fuel. The digital fuel gauge showed 0.000. I figured the airstream had sucked out all the fuel, including that from the engine tanks. I didn't have much time for debate. But then it dawned on me – it can't be! The fuel in the engine tanks couldn't have been sucked out because there's a one-way valve. I have to have 1100 pounds somewhere.

I worked like a machine. Automatic movements. No fear. No worry. I knew just one thing: as long as the aircraft was flying, I was flying with it. Even if all I had left was the stick in my hand.

We began to descend for a landing. I had to check the minimum speed at which the aircraft was still controllable and lowered my wheels. I asked Number Two whether they had come down and he confirmed all three. I started to slow down as gently as I could; I knew I'd have a problem when the aircraft reached low speed. When it hit 250 knots the aircraft went into a downward spin to the right. At this point one wing wasn't enough.

After one turn I decided this was it. We had to get out right away. But I tried one last thing; I went into full afterburner, figuring my only chance was to gain speed. It worked. When the speed rose to 270 knots I was able to regain control. From this point on I would have to get used to the idea that I was going to land at twice the allowable speed. I lowered my emergency landing hook. G panicked in the rear cockpit. 'My landing hook light isn't on!' I answered him firmly, 'No problem. Mine's lit.' The two of us were under such pressure it didn't even occur to us that there is no landing hook light in the rear cockpit ...

I crossed the threshold at 270–280 knots and touched down at 260. At first everything seemed okay. We hit the first cable and the deceleration was quite strong. We kept racing along and then I realized the cable had played out to the end and due to our speed it had simply torn the landing hook right from the aircraft. But my speed had already dropped by 100 knots and I was already more relaxed; 150 knots is almost a normal landing speed and this could be handled with the brakes.

I called the tower to raise the net, but got no answer. I called again and again until the word 'net' turned into a scream. They were in shock, or whatever, but when they saw a one-winged aircraft pass before their eyes they realized they had to do something. So they raised the net. Our brakes stopped us ten metres away.

I opened the canopy and extended my arm back to shake hands with G. I turned my head a little and my smile made way for a shout of surprise: 'No wing!' This was the first time I really grasped what had happened.

We got out of the aircraft completely stunned. I still couldn't comprehend a thing and a huge, dumb smile was all over my face. We were immediately surrounded by pilots from the base who had seen an emergency landing and had come to hear what had happened. They came from the side with the wing and wondered why we had landed in the middle of an exercise, as if we had done so for no reason at all. When they moved to the other side of the aircraft a moment of astonished silence took hold. N was the first to speak. 'Tell me,' he said, turning to me, 'can I switch to F-15s?'

The day after an accident they usually let a pilot fly a

regular flight so he won't dwell too much on what happened and become afraid. The day of my accident it was my turn for night alert. After the debriefing everyone disappeared and left me at the squadron. Just like that. No ceremonies, no psychology. The next day I made a regular flight. I felt completely comfortable. I had always had complete confidence in the F-15; now it was even stronger. The F-15 is an aircraft with superior controls and I think this is why it kept flying with just one wing. I mean, it wasn't magic; all I did was do things right.

The Skyhawk pilot got off lightly enough: a few burns and some holes in his parachute from the fire. A few days later I visited him in the hospital. When he recovered he went back to flying.

Two and a half months after the accident the aircraft was once more in the air. They checked over the spars and installed a new wing. I made the test flight. The original wing, by the way, was found not far from the scene of the collision. It had simply been torn from the fuselage and had fallen in one piece to the ground.

The folks from McDonnell Douglas, manufacturers of the F-15, found it hard to believe the story. They had issued a detailed report that determined, from an aerodynamic point of view, that it would be impossible to fly and land with one wing. One of our pilots used a visit by a senior executive of the firm to ask him how much of a wing could fall off and the aircraft still fly. He answered, a third; beyond a third the aircraft won't fly. The pilot couldn't hold back and said, 'Come. Come and see something.'

It's hard even for me to digest this strange occurrence. From time to time I think about every aspect: I replay my actions and consider what would have happened if ... and what could have happened if not. I figure these kinds of thoughts pass through the minds of everyone who flies a lot in the Air Force. Every pilot has 'almost died' like this a number of times. A close call in a dogfight gives the same feeling of almost dying. I didn't feel that I had come any closer this time. As time goes by I remember this flight more as the story of an event, and less of feelings, horror and fear. The truth is I had almost no time to be afraid. I was busy working things and my brain was functioning on just one channel: how not to have to bail out.

The only thing left alive in my memory is the mistaken feeling that the flight went on for a long time. I was amazed to discover that only five minutes passed from the time of the collision to the landing. Afterwards I heard this happens to many. Difficult situations seem to stretch out in the minds of those who go through them – much farther than their real time spans.

A little while after the accident we went to the US for simulator training. We were waiting for one of the guys near the airfield in El Paso, sitting in a car, and we saw two Skyhawks coming in. I looked at the aircraft and said, 'I think the one behind is going to crash on landing.' When I said the Skyhawk was going to crash, everyone stopped what he was doing and waited. The first one landed with no problem. The second landed and crashed. Its landing gear broke and it exploded and the pilot ejected fifty metres away from us. That was it. No one wanted to come near me anymore.

Chapter 35
TO CAPTIVITY AND BACK, IN ONE DAY

In November 1983, Lieutenant Colonel M's Kfir was hit over Lebanon, and he bailed out south of Beirut. Fortunately he fell into the hands of the Lebanese Army; he was released from 'captivity' the same day and returned home.

While turning I felt a kind of blow underneath the aircraft. There was no sign in the cockpit of my having been hit. For a moment I wanted to believe that nothing had happened, but inside a dark feeling of anger, disappointment and fear began to well up. This was it. It had happened to me. I'd been hit.

The mission had been a strike against targets at Hammana, north of the Beirut–Damascus highway and on the mountains near the descent to Beka'a. The whole morning had been spent preparing for the raid. The squadron was very busy. For a long time we had not made an operational sortie and our turn had finally come. Coincidentally, Major General Gad Navon, the chief rabbi of the IDF, had visited us the same day. He was told we were going out on a raid and he immediately offered a blessing with deep feeling. The next day he called me, totally agitated. 'Rabbi,' I told him, 'the blessing apparently wasn't enough.'

Ahead of us, over Lebanon, there was a thin layer of cloud at 14,000 feet. We had to drop down lower than planned, opening ourselves up to the possibility of early detection by terrorist forces. I descended below the cloud layer and waited for the first formation to complete its attack.

During this time I heard one of the pilots report on anti-aircraft fire and missiles in the area.

It's my turn to attack. The target area is covered with smoke from the strike by the previous formation. I locate 'my' house, though in the briefing it had looked a little different. I'm not sure if I've identified the right target and I decide not to release my bombs on the first pass; first make sure from close up that this is indeed my objective. The building is on the edge of the village, near other houses, and I'm afraid I made too hasty an identification. I go into the pass and exit in a left turn, intending to go in again. And then it happens. An anti-aircraft shell strikes the fuselage. There's hardly any chance that a shell like this will hit. But it hits me.

I announce over the radio that I've been hit, head for the coast, and release everything that's on the aircraft, bombs and drop tanks. I open up the throttle and decide to climb. There are some fifteen miles to the coast and I hope I'll be able to go on until the sea. Climbing to altitude, I tensely monitor the aircraft's performance. At first all's well: the engine works, the instruments work, everything's normal. But very quickly the warning light goes on for one of the hydraulic systems and I feel as if I've been dealt a stinging slap on the face.

My Number Two is a young pilot and this is his first operational sortie. I call him over the radio and in a voice choked with shame ask him to check me over. He pulls in close and reports I've got damage to a wing. The painful shame is so powerful that it obliterates fear.

The controls start getting stiff and a gallery of tales about Phantom pilots in Vietnam, who would suddenly stall out and crash, go through my mind. I announce over the radio that it looks like I might have to bail out and from this moment I know it's going to be bad. Just like in the novels, all kinds of flashbacks run through my head: I see myself in situations from days long gone; images and faces appear before my eyes. I think about Gil Fogel, imprisoned in Syria. Did he feel this same fear mixed with anger? Did he feel like that, from this moment, his life would never be the same?

The nose pitches up hard and the controls freeze. Already out of control, the aircraft goes into a downward spin like a slow carousel. The view goes round like in a horror movie: the Beka'a, the coastline, Halde, Beirut. Occasionally the nose drops, and my heart skips a beat – maybe it's still possible to regain control. Maybe I'll be able to get out of this yet. But no, it's clear I'm sitting in an airplane that's no longer an airplane and it's only a matter of time.

I don't remember what I was thinking the moment I ejected. I only remember I did all the right things, but with a smouldering anger – at myself, at the world, at the aircraft. Yes, yes, at the aircraft. This was the squadron's prize aircraft, with the best hits and never a breakdown. An airplane so good that I took it for myself. It was 'mine'. And now the two of us were ending our career together.

The ejection goes quite smoothly, though I'll feel it in my back for a few days to come. I take a tremendous whack and in the background hear the fading noise of the airplane. After a few seconds it's totally quiet. It's 2:30 in the afternoon, a clear autumn day.

I'm hanging beneath a parachute 4500 feet above south Beirut. I know it's all over and that events will now be controlling me and not I events. I look down and see I'm going to land on a main street heading south from the city. As I get lower, things are clearer. I see houses with large balconies, empty fields, and lots in between. The thing that bothers me most right now is that I'm going to land on one of these balconies. I try to steer the parachute away from the houses and notice that people are already gathering below. Out of the corner of my eye I see the aircraft spinning into the ground.

I touch down gently in a field on the roadside. Right away a group of soldiers draws near. I tick off the possibilities: terrorists? Christians? Amal? Syrians? I see their uniforms are very neat and this is somewhat reassuring. Well, these aren't terrorists.

The soldiers hold the crowds back, encircle me and then put me in a green BMW. My first question is, 'Who are you?' In English they answer, 'It's all right we're from the Lebanese Army.' I hope it's true but decide to expect the worst. Don't believe a word; don't be too hopeful; don't be seduced.

We speed crazily through the streets and alleys, their jeep in front, to their headquarters, where a local physician checks me over. They show me to an officer who chances by and a number of times I emphasize where I'm from so he'll remember he saw an Israeli pilot.

Already I have gloomy thoughts that this is the beginning of three years of captivity. I expect the worst. Actually, I don't know what to expect. Every motion, every sentence is suspect.

Looking back, I had no reason to be suspicious. I was shown extraordinary courtesy. I was presented to Lebanese officers at the headquarters; they spoke with me a little, but only in generalities, as if the whole thing didn't hold much interest for them.

After an hour or two they tell me they've reported about me to the Israeli authorities. I don't believe it. Though they've been behaving properly, my suspicions don't recede. Again and again I repeat to myself: don't believe them; don't be suckered. For this reason I'm afraid to accept their proposal that I undergo a checkup at a hospital. I want to remain at the headquarters at any price. As for them, they constantly try to reassure me. But I'm still thinking it's all deception, that this courtesy is just to allay my fears before imprisonment.

Under cover of darkness they set out to take me to the hospital, dress me in a tracksuit, blindfold me and put me in an ambulance. Again, a wild trip through the streets until the ambulance suddenly stops. A flat tyre. We're stuck in the middle of the street and everyone panics. I can now look on this as a kind of comic relief, as if a skilled director has momentarily halted a horror movie and stuck in something ridiculous to break the tension.

Another ambulance shows up and takes us to the hospital. I'm put in a closed room, with a guard in the hall. They take a few x-rays and determine that I have a pressure fracture.

We return to their HQ, where they happily inform me they're about to send me back to Israel. I'm still afraid to hope. A short time later they tell me, 'That's it, you're going back.' My heart misses beats from emotion, but I keep a straight face. Just don't show you believe them. If it's a trick, at least they won't have the satisfaction of feeling they've put one over on you. I convince myself not to believe them. Till the last minute.

On the way they remove my blindfold and let me see a little of Beirut. Again we switch cars. We get on a highway and I see we're going north.

When I'm handed over to Israeli forces the tension

189

vanishes. A few of our people are waiting for me and finally I hear Hebrew. The moment is so emotional I can't put it into words.

On the way back to Israel in the helicopter, I insisted on one thing: I wasn't going home in a Lebanese tracksuit, so I changed into flight coveralls. We landed at Tel Hashomer, where the GOC Air Force, my base commander and the guys from the squadron were waiting. In the hospital they wanted me to stay for tests and observation, but there was nothing to discuss – I felt I had to get back to my base the same night.

I arrived at the wing at 2 a.m. Everyone was waiting with welcoming placards, tears and hugs, and they gave me a reception in the officers' club. The next day it all seemed to have been a dream.

Chapter 36
1200 MILES FROM HOME

The bombing of the PLO headquarters in Tunis on 1 October 1985 was one of the longest-range strikes ever undertaken by the Israel Air Force. Lieutenant Colonel M was one of the pilots who took part.

This was the kind of flight you make once in your life; you can't screw up because you're carrying a tremendous burden of expectations. This time the burden was particularly heavy; the flight was being called a mission on behalf of the nation.

The pre-sortie preparations were tremendous. The far-off objective required sophisticated and strict logistics. Every problem led to another and every solution begat a question mark. We tried to picture every expected malfunction; for each one we prepared an answer. The operation was composed of many different factors and details and its success depended on harmony. Messing up on one level could have brought everything down.

Despite the sensitive nature of the flight, it was decided not to assemble an all-star lineup of pilots, but rather to have the various squadrons assign suitable fliers. Mission details were even more of a secret than usual – I was let in on the mission four days before it was executed. Most of the squadron personnel had to be alert and under great tension without our being able to tell them what it was all about.

The pilots were organized into work crews, each of which detailed a specific part of the flight; there were no special physical preparations. We only made sure not to show up too tired for the flight itself. As to what we ate and drank before the flight, life was a lot simpler than was portrayed by the press. We weren't aided by a nutrition expert; the 'expert' was an administration officer. One pilot was responsible for provisions, and supplied each of us with a quarter-kilogram of dried fruits and a few containers of grape juice. We avoided coffee so as to prevent undue bladder pressure during the long flight that awaited us. A few pilots took along warm clothes in case they had to bail out; this worry was always prevalent.

We knew this was beyond routine security; it was a mission of political and historical importance. We knew the bombing of the terrorist headquarters would be a real and extraordinary blow that would make a lot of media noise. And all this was accompanied by worry. Would it all come off as planned? Would something come up on the way which we had not anticipated? I didn't get into the aircraft with feelings of guilt or hatred, but with the desire to give it my all. There was no doubt the decision had been correct and just. I concentrated on the execution alone, which required less emotion, just straight thinking.

We went down to the aircraft an hour before take-off, checked things over, checked them again and checked them once more. The technicians circled us, eyeing us with worry and much hope. From personal experience I knew that the people most affected by the loss of a pilot are the ground crew.

At start-up everyone was anxious that there would be no last-minute malfunctions and that they wouldn't be forced to abort the take-off. Every check was accompanied by fear; those with experience know that until take-off nothing is certain; and those with even more experience know that nothing is certain afterwards.

The aircraft were very heavy, loaded with fuel and bombs; we taxied very gingerly. The whole base was out there watching us. I counted the aircraft taking off and hoped to count the same number on landing.

The navigation computer showed a figure the likes of which had never before appeared on Israeli displays: 1200 miles – and the whole way I'd be alone. No one with whom to share the tension, the fear, and the joy that would come afterwards.

The weather was on our side the whole way. At the scheduled hour we met up with refuelling aircraft, exactly according to plan. Satisfaction for a moment and then the last part: the strike. The target – Hammam e-Shatt – was on the gulf; the whole gulf was covered with clouds. Miraculously, there was no cloud at all over the target.

The tension rose, blood was infused with an extra dose of adrenaline and powers of concentration reached their peak.

All phases of the execution – locating the target, identifying it, the bombing, the hits – went almost 100 per cent according to plan. I came out of my pass and saw my bombs had hit the target accurately; heavy smoke was rising from the objective.

From a bird's eye view you don't see little details or notice human forms. The picture looks nothing like what you see afterwards on the television. You only see that you've hit the target.

And then came a tremendous release of tension. I let out a great roar in the cockpit. The feelings were mixed: you saw that you left behind great ruin but knew everything was done perfectly. And this is what everyone had wanted – the planners, the doers – really the whole nation.

I began to think about the way home. In the air I had already done a kind of initial debriefing with myself on the mission's execution. I was stunned when I realized there were another 1200 miles to go. And the road seemed long. Very long. Time stood still; the thirst and hunger were annoying; the oxygen mask pressed the sides of my nose; my bottom hurt; my bladder was full. Suddenly there was time to deal with the flight's little annoyances.

Returning home this time was much more meaningful. All at once I saw the shores of Israel in a different way. My spirits rose like never before, quite unlike returning to Israel on other flights, or returning from abroad. A completely new feeling.

As a sign of appreciation to the ground crews we made the traditional buzz over the base and then landed. The whole squadron awaited us, everyone who had followed the operation without knowing exactly what it was about. Everybody was excited, including us. I descended from the aircraft and only after I noticed there were no bombs aboard did I begin to digest what had happened. Yes, yes, I had been there.

Only once I had returned did I really begin to absorb what had happened. The squadron had added another page to history.

Chapter 37
HANGING FROM THE
LANDING SKID

On 16 October 1986, during a routine raid over Lebanon, an Israel Air Force Phantom suffered a technical malfunction; one of its bombs exploded too close beneath the aircraft's belly. The two crewmen bailed out. The pilot was rescued by a pair of Cobra attack helicopters, with him hanging by his hands from the landing skid of one of the aircraft, crewed by Major A and Captain H.

Phantom pilot It was a regular workday at the factory and the next day the whole family was to leave for a week's vacation. At 11:30 in the morning they suddenly called from the squadron and asked me to come down as soon as possible. During the afternoon we went out to bomb a terrorist camp about five kilometres southeast of Sidon. At around 16:40 we were over the target. We went in for the strike. I pressed the bomb release and the bombs began to fall away with tremendous acceleration – half a second and it seemed half the load had hit the ground.

And then the explosion. Something right out of the movies. I was sure I had been killed. I heard a terrific boom and could see nothing – not my hands, not the instruments, not the airplane. Just fire; a glittering. I felt as if I was simply coming apart and vaporizing; lying on my back, spinning upwards, being taken to my forefathers ...

The red turned to black, which even further strengthened the feeling that I was dead. I thought how I had always wanted to see what death looked like. Fine, so this was what it looked like ... I was very calm and relaxed. I wasn't afraid. And then I awoke from this euphoria; someone or something – I didn't know how or what – pulled on me and to my surprise I saw myself hanging from a parachute. I was surprised to discover I was alive at all and I said 'Thanks,' very nicely. The passage was quite stark: from superiority and great control of an airplane to tremendous disadvantage in the control of whatever wind there was.

I swore in Arabic and thought there was no place worse than this to bail out. A real hornet's nest. There was a mixture of explosions and gunfire and ambulances. I saw the gunshots going by underneath me.

The wind carried me until I smashed against the slope of a wadi; I fell into an awful thicket of something like raspberries. This was the best hiding place I had ever come across in my life. I couldn't help being reminded of all the games of hide and seek I played in my childhood, but this time I felt I was participating in a real game, for keeps. The ravine was totally covered by thistles and it was impossible to walk through it. I crawled into the densest part I could find and hid beneath three metres of raspberries and half a metre of leaves.

Maj A, the Cobra pilot It was clear they had scrambled us to silence the source of fire. During the scramble phase we headed for the area and were told we'd receive our instructions later. We flew toward Rosh Hanikra, on the frontier, listening to what was happening over the radio. After Rosh Hanikra, about a kilometre and a half out to sea, I tried out the cannon because I had been having a problem with the helicopter's electrical system.

After a relatively short time we received instructions to go in. As we crossed the coastline into Lebanon the sun began to go down. We didn't expect any special problems.

Phantom pilot I was lying in the bushes. I had no doubts they'd catch me. I told myself if I could only try and delay this, but felt I wouldn't be able to, that they'd come a lot sooner because things were deteriorating. The terrorists had seen where I had landed and started coming down from all directions.

They fired at the bushes on the way and closed in. I made

myself smaller and smaller, curled up and quiet. I think they approached to within a hundred metres of me. Due to the depth and steepness of the wadi it was hard to make it down without broken arms and legs. These were twenty or thirty very tough and very long minutes; I had a watch, and all the time I kept looking at it.

The moment of capture, which I was sure would arrive, really frightened me because it could have ended in death. It's a moment that's hard to accept. I thought all kinds of things; for example, I'd finally lose weight. I tried to look at the bright side of captivity because it was clear that this was what faced me. I thought how bad it would be for my family. But Air Force helicopter gunships suddenly arrived and began strafing and this silenced the terrorists around me. I think they fled, because I heard the voices getting farther away.

Things started looking up. The feeling that the whole Air Force was behind me was tremendous. It changed the whole picture. I saw they were willing to do everything – strafing, keeping an eye on me – while placing themselves in danger. I was proud. Despair slowly turned to hope. I told myself that Metulla was the closest place in Israel and that I'd have to consider making it there. I thought only the first kilometre would be a problem, the moving between the villages. After that there'd just be the walk. I had no idea what would happen. I thought about the possibility of their coming to rescue me, but it seemed to be wishful thinking that a helicopter could get in there. One bullet would be enough to bring it down.

It was already dark. At this point I discovered that my ear was torn, apparently from the ejection. It didn't hurt, but I felt like there was a four-piece fig leaf where my ear should have been. I came out from under the raspberries and leaves and opened a kind of window so I'd be able to see what was happening outside. It was then that I heard the noise from the helicopters. I looked out of the 'window' and saw them flying around up above.

Maj A We descended deep towards the pilot. I shouted that there was contact with the survivor. Everyone understood that this was the important thing.

Capt H, the second Cobra pilot We got ready to make the

rescue. This meant getting the pilot, who was inside a very deep canyon, and having him climb out, because it was impossible to go all the way in. We explained to him what we were going to do and told him to climb the wadi's north side as far as he could.

Phantom pilot The minute they told me they were going to come in to take me out on their landing skids I knew there was going to be a rescue and I was elated. This idea seemed okay – I didn't think there was any other way. It didn't even interest me if there would be room, it wasn't at all relevant: I was ready to make it out of there on a child's scooter, as long as it would fly.

Getting out of the wadi to where they could reach me was very difficult. The northern slope was the steepest, more like a wall, and I couldn't climb it. I couldn't get clear of the raspberries. My feet got stuck and there was nowhere to grab hold. I tried to go up in all sorts of places; I trampled the raspberries and bulled my way through like a rhinoceros. I looked for places to put my hands and feet, to get higher, but couldn't do it. My gloves were lost in ejecting, but nothing hurt. Apparently nature saw to that.

In the end I decided that I was wasting my strength for nothing, and told them I was going to try the other side. The main thing was to get out. The southern slope was not as steep and with great effort I was able to make the climb. I was helped along by the thistles, which I didn't think would hold even a chicken. My feet slipped; I climbed like Mickey Mouse, holding the radio by turns in my pocket, hand or mouth, clenched between my teeth. I made fifteen to twenty metres in almost a quarter of an hour. I made it to where there was a kind of rocky incline standing out in the wadi, and saw that in front and to the rear the sides were wide enough for a helicopter. That's where I stopped. Suddenly I looked at the Cobras and saw they were pulling out! My heart sank.

Maj A Number One started to go into the wadi; he stopped to hover 300 feet above the estimated spot and waited for the pilot. We were right behind, covering him. He suddenly heard the sharp sound of metal on metal and his controls went stiff. He reported this and said he was getting out. That very second my electricity went out in the rear cockpit. I thought to myself that we had taken off with a malfunction and now it had got worse. My first feeling was one of despair because Number One had left the survivor and we, without electricity, couldn't go into the wadi. And here we were departing the area and leaving the pilot alone. Number One turned south, with us right behind, and during this time I ran a check of the cockpit and saw the electricity was working! I needed another fifteen seconds or so to understand exactly what had happened and then, with an instinctive movement, I shot my hand towards the right switch and the electricity came back on. The whole process took about half a minute. Number One said we'd stay and manage the business.

We turned back towards the Phantom pilot and identified his position quickly enough. We couldn't see him because it was dark. In addition to this, we were low on fuel and what went through my mind was that we had to make the rescue now or we'd run out of gas.

The minute we made our decision we no longer thought about the fuel. We spoke once more with the pilot and told him we were coming to get him. We made two circuits above him to see his exact location in the wadi, with him directing us beautifully. We went in for the final circuit north of the wadi and they began firing at us with light weapons. The pilot suggested we come in lower, beneath the lips of the wadi, so that the fire would pass above us. That's exactly what we did and it worked fine.

The pilot was a real man about it. Unbelievably cool. He spoke with indifference as if he was sitting in the bath. We felt we were dealing with a responsible man who knew what he was talking about and saying it right. We went in for a final low-level circuit, descending into the wadi, which seemed okay. At that moment I thought of the Jerusalem hills, which have similar wadis.

Capt H We made a pass at medium level, with the pilot giving our distance. You could say we just brought the helicopter to him. The rest he did himself. He performed beyond expectation. When we were about ten metres away I saw him standing on a cliff.

Phantom pilot I stood up and waved my hands at the helicopter until the pilot saw me. I directed him until we stood face to face – and then I saw Captain H pointing at me.

I really saw the movement of his hand. At this point, when they had come to me, I finally lost my cool.

Maj A We planned to open the door to the ammunition drum and seat the pilot there. But the moment we stopped to hover the pilot wouldn't wait. Sitting behind, I saw a black figure run towards the helicopter, leap and disappear. I thought he had failed to catch hold and ended back up in the wadi.

Phantom pilot I grabbed the strut that held the landing skid to the helicopter and hooked myself on to the skid with my armpits. This seemed the best way, natural and quick. I didn't want any problems out there, as the proximity of the wadi's walls made it dangerous for the helicopter to stay there. They hovered so that the landing skid stood at chest height and all I had to do was grab hold. With one hand I held on to the skid and with the other I held on to the radio, into which I shouted, 'Go, go!'

Capt H He shouted so loudly that I heard him without the radio. We decided to move out. We couldn't fly too fast because almost all of him was dangling in mid-air. I opened the door and the whole time watched to see that he didn't fall. We climbed westward at low speed and passed over a village sitting on a hill in front of us. We felt very exposed, a very unpleasant feeling.

Maj A The question that bothered us most at this point was whether they'd fire at us from the village and whether the pilot would hold on. I feared he wouldn't have the strength. We flew over the lit village and anyone who raised his head would have seen the pilot dangling, with his legs swinging in the air. I said we couldn't fly like this any more. I dropped the nose and speeded up. I shouted to Captain H, 'See if he's still hanging there.'

Phantom pilot I didn't feel like I was going to fall. It wasn't hard to hold on – it would have been a lot more difficult to go into captivity. I felt I could hold on like this for a long time, but assumed the pilots in the Cobra realized I wasn't in the best of shape and were going to land shortly. When we flew above the village a burst of fire passed below us. But nothing worried me. I knew I was out! I was hooked up to an IAF helicopter and that was it. Who could get me off there?

Capt H We flew towards the coast with the goal of landing in that general vicinity and seating the pilot on the ammunition step so we'd be able to fly back to Israel more safely. We tried to land on the way; we found a fine area with oil storage tanks. The place looked quiet enough and we stopped to hover.

Phantom pilot I jumped down and then someone fired. I wasn't frightened because it was high and wasn't aimed at us. They dropped down to a height of half a metre and I quickly sat myself down on the skid as if on a motorcycle; my back was towards the direction of flight and I hugged the arch that was supporting me so I wouldn't fly off behind the helicopter. Sitting like this seemed most natural.

I sat myself down and they took off; there was no need to speak because the chemistry between us was wonderful. They were people who knew what they were doing. It was quite comfortable for me to sit like this; I leaned my left shoulder against the helicopter and the wind pinned me to the support. At that point my ear hurt because the wind caused it to flap. I covered it with my right hand and every time I felt Captain H opening the helicopter door I signalled him with the hand that was covering my ear that everything was all right. I was ready to continue in this fashion all the way home, but we suddenly landed. At first I didn't know what they were doing.

Maj A They suddenly informed us that a rescue helicopter was nearby. We turned on our formation lights and he was flying behind us. Although the pilot seemed to be sitting all right we were afraid he might fall, or that he wasn't feeling well. We decided to set him down on the beach and try to transfer him to the rescue helicopter. We explained our intentions to the rescue helicopter and when there were no more lights along the coast we decided to land. We went over the Litani estuary, north of Tyre, which seemed very quiet; we stopped to hover and the pilot got off. Suddenly I saw he was none other than the instructor I had admired so much at the Flight Academy. An awful shudder went through my whole body.

Phantom pilot I didn't know where I was or what to do. I didn't understand why they had landed. I signalled them with my hand: What's happened? And then sudden fire, apparently

201

an RPG. In the flash I saw the rescue helicopter and understood everything. Captain H signalled me to get back on quickly and I sat myself down on the helicopter in the same fashion and began thinking about everything that had happened and what was going to happen. I wasn't tired and felt nothing physical except for my ear. I thought about whether I had done enough to get my navigator out and how good it would be if he were sitting on the other side of the helicopter.

Capt H We decided that from this point on we would fly straight to Rosh Hanikra. We flew over the sea at a height of 100 feet and a speed of 100 knots. The rescue helicopter escorted us. We arrived at Rosh Hanikra and stopped to hover at the spot closest to the cliff.

Phantom pilot The moment we landed I didn't have the strength to stand on my feet. Suddenly and all at once, everything was over and came undone. I tried to stand, but simply couldn't. I sat down on the rocks. The rescue helicopter flew me to Rambam Hospital, there I first asked myself whether they knew about this at home. I saw a telephone and remembered I could use it, but my wife showed up before I could. They sewed up my ear. I had a lot of scratches from the raspberries on all the exposed parts of my body and my face was burned from the explosion. (When my helmet had flown off I was still in the fire.) The next day everything hurt, but after three days everything had worn off and passed. Now the only scars were inside.

I call the rescue operation a combination of coincidence and luck. It was a very fragile chain whose glass links simply held. Any little thing could have prevented my rescue. We were very lucky. Every incident led to either tremendous hope or despair – there were a lot of ups and downs. That I was able to help out Captain H and Major A – thanks to them I'm here – was just another bit of luck in that same chain. Those Cobra pilots were without doubt the real heroes. When they entered the wadi I really admired them, but I had a terrible fear that something would happen to them because of me. I only found out the next day that it was Major A, who had been my pupil, that had rescued me. I think this turned out nicely; it closed a circle.

I think I've really changed in terms of how I look at life.

The proportions have changed. What were once big things are today unimportant and uninteresting. There are influences that remain forever and things that pass with time. After what happened I decided that I had not known myself at all. I had always thought I was an instinctive person and didn't know I could be this cool. I was very pleasantly surprised although I think anyone else would have behaved the same way.

My thoughts right now are about the explosion and what happened. All the time I think about what happened to my navigator, and what they're doing to him. It's very hard.

The ejection and rescue are not things you forget about. One could say this is a psychological wound that would be a lot smaller if the navigator were here. And also, if this had happened in the middle of some massive war, I would feel a lot better because this would have been a small incident – for me and the whole country. I really didn't like being a 'star'. Not even for a moment did I feel like a hero.

Sphere now offers an exciting range of quality titles by both established and new authors. All of the books in this series are available from:
Sphere Books,
Cash Sales Department,
P.O. Box 11,
Falmouth,
Cornwall TR10 9EN.

Alternatively you may fax your order to the above address. Fax No. 0326 376423.

Payments can be made as follows: Cheque, postal order (payable to Macdonald & Co (Publishers) Ltd) or by credit cards, Visa/Access. Do not send cash or currency. UK customers and B.F.P.O.: please send a cheque or postal order (no currency), and allow £1.00 for postage and packing for the first book, plus 50p for the second book, 30p for each additional book up to a maximum charge of £3.00 (7 books plus).

Overseas customers including Ireland, please allow £2.00 for postage and packing for the first book, plus £1.00 for the second book, plus 50p for each additional book.

NAME (Block Letters)..

ADDRESS ....

....

☐ I enclose my remittance for_____

☐ I wish to pay by Access/Visa Card

Number | | | | | | | | | | | | | | | |

Card Expiry Date | | | | |